ETHICS
A Contemporary Introduction

Harry J. Gensler

London and New York

First published 1998
by Routledge
11 New Fetter Lane, London EC4P 4EE

Simultaneously published in the USA and Canada
by Routledge
29 West 35th Street, New York, NY 10001

Reprinted 2000

Routledge is an imprint of the Taylor & Francis Group

Typeset in Aldus Roman
by the author
Printed and bound in Great Britain by
TJ International Ltd, Padstow, Cornwall

British Library Cataloguing in Publication Data
A catalogue record for this book is available from the British Library.

Library of Congress Cataloging-in-Publication Data
A catalogue record for this book has been requested.

ISBN: 0–415–15624–6 (hbk)
ISBN: 0–415–15625–4 (pbk)

Contents

Chapter 5: Emotivism   58

Chapter 6: Prescriptivism   71

Chapter 7: Consistency   84

Chapter 8: The Golden Rule   103

Chapter 9: Moral Rationality   122

Chapter 10: Consequentialism   138

Preface

Ethics: A Contemporary Introduction introduces the issues and controversies of contemporary moral philosophy. It covers many of the basic metaethical and normative views. It relates these to specific issues, particularly racism, moral education, and abortion.

I wrote this book, not for a general audience, but for undergraduate college students, with their interests and struggles. I aimed at students who have had one or two previous philosophy courses.

I've tried to relate the various views to the student's own growth into adulthood. While children are expected to parrot the moral views they were taught, whether by parents or by society, adults need to think out moral issues for themselves. But how can we think out moral issues in the wisest and most rational way? I take this to be the central issue of moral philosophy.

A typical chapter begins with a clear, forceful, and often very plausible defense of a view by a fictional student. The reader is thus invited to take the view seriously and to understand it on its own terms. Problems and objections come later. In all this, I'm trying to encourage the reader to think critically – to clarify a view and look for problems, instead of just accepting whatever sounds good.

In writing the book, I've tried to be clear and concise. I've tried to use examples that are meaningful to students. And I've tried to show how different approaches can affect our lives. While I've argued strongly against many views, I've tried to be fair-minded. I'm concerned, not that students agree with me, but that they think out the issues more deeply and arrive at approaches that they can live by in a consistent way.

I've provided various study aids. These include boxes for key ideas, highlighted technical terms (with a glossary for definitions), chapter summaries, study questions, suggested readings, computer exercises, and Internet Web links. Students who use these study aids will more easily grasp the complexities of moral philosophy.

While I've aimed this book at students, it also should be of interest to the general reader. The direct, nontechnical language should make the book understandable to a wide range of people.

For further ideas on how to use this book, teachers can explore the Computer Exercises appendix (especially Section E) and Routledge's Web page (http://www.routledge.com/routledge/philosophy/cip/ethics.htm) on the book.

I thank five philosophers who read the first draft of this book for Routledge and made many very helpful suggestions: Robert Arrington (Georgia State University), Ben Bradley (University of Massachusetts at Amherst), Jeanette Kennett (Monash University), Mark Walker (University of Birmingham), and especially Thomas Carson (Loyola University of Chicago). I also thank my students for their many ideas on how to improve the text.

I hope that students and others enjoy the book. And I hope that it helps them to think more clearly about one of life's central questions: "How can we form our moral beliefs in the wisest and most rational way?"

Harry J. Gensler
John Carroll University
University Heights
Cleveland, OH 44118 USA

http://www.jcu.edu/philosophy/gensler

Introduction

Introduction

When we do moral philosophy, we reflect on how we ought to live. We ask what principles we ought to live by – and why we should follow these principles instead of others. We study various views and try to sort through them rationally.

In this chapter, we'll first consider the general nature of philosophy. Then we'll focus on the main issues of *moral* philosophy and why we should be concerned about them.

A.   Philosophy

To do **philosophy** is to reason about the ultimate questions of life – questions such as these:

- Is there a God?
- Are our actions free or determined?
- Are humans completely explainable in material terms?
- How and what can we know?
- What is the nature and methodology of moral judgments?
- What principles ought we to live by?

Such questions are difficult and controversial; we struggle with them. Often our answers are confused or implicit. Our answers, whether good or bad, give us a perspective for thinking and acting – a "world view."

Philosophy deals with ultimate questions by *reasoning* about them. We first try to get clear on what the question is asking. Then we consider the range of possible answers. We criticize each one as brutally as we can, trying to uncover problems; and we eliminate views that lead to absurdities. We look for the most adequate of the remaining views. If we can't completely resolve the issue, at least we can hope to arrive at a well thought-out answer.

Other disciplines can deal with beliefs about ultimate questions. We can study the *history* of such beliefs, their *psychological* causes or stages, or how they relate to *literature* or *religion*. These approaches are valuable, but they don't replace *philosophy* – which reasons and debates about the ultimate questions of life.

B.   Logical reasoning

Before we consider moral philosophy, we'd do well to review a few ideas about reasoning and logic.

Reasoning in philosophy resembles reasoning in other areas. We often reason about things like who committed the murder, what car to buy, whether there is a greatest prime number, or how to cure cancer. As we approach these issues, we clarify the question and gather background information. We review what others have said. We consider alternative views and objections to them. We make distinctions and weigh pros and cons. The climax of the process is when we take a stand and try to justify it. We explain that the answer must be such and such, and we point to other facts to justify our answer. This is **logical reasoning**, where we go from premises to a conclusion.

To reason logically is to conclude something from something else. For example, we conclude that the butler committed the murder from the beliefs that (1) either the butler or the maid did it, and (2) the maid didn't do it. If we put reasoning into words, we get an **argument** – a set of statements consisting of premises and a conclusion:

Either the butler or the maid did it.	B or M
The maid didn't do it.	Not-M
∴ The butler did it.	∴ B

(Here "∴" is short for "therefore.") This argument is **valid**, which means that the conclusion follows logically from the premises. If the premises are true, then the conclusion must be true. So if we can be confident of the premises, then we can be confident that the butler did it.

Calling an argument *valid* claims that the conclusion follows from the premises; it doesn't say that the premises are true. To prove something, we also need true premises. If we give clearly true premises from which our conclusion logically follows, then we've proved our conclusion.

Philosophy involves much logical reasoning. The most common form of logical reasoning in philosophy is when we attack a view P by arguing that it leads to an absurdity Q:

If P is true, then Q would be true.
Q is false.
∴ P is false.

As we examine a view, we consider its logical implications and look for flaws. If we find clearly false implications, then we've shown that the view is false. And if we find highly doubtful implications, then we've cast doubt on the view. Either way, we've made progress.

As we develop our philosophical views, reasoning and personal commitment are both important. Reasoning alone won't resolve all the disputes. After considering the arguments on both sides, we have to make up our own minds. But if we pick a view with strong objections, then we have to respond to these.

C.   Moral philosophy

To do **moral philosophy** (or **ethics**) is to reason about the ultimate questions of morality. We've mentioned the two key questions:

Metaethics: What is the nature and methodology of moral judgments?	**Normative Ethics:** What principles ought we to live by?

Moral philosophy accordingly has two main branches.

Metaethics studies the nature and methodology of moral judgments. It asks questions like: What do "good" and "ought" mean? Are there moral truths? How can we justify or rationally defend beliefs about right and wrong?

A metaethical view normally has two parts. One part is about the nature of moral judgments; this is often a definition of "good." The other part is about methodology; this tells how to select moral principles. For example, cultural relativism says:

- "Good" means "socially approved."
- Pick out your moral principles by following what your society approves of.

Cultural relativism bases morality on social conventions. Other views may base it on personal feelings, God's will, or self-evident truths.

Normative ethics studies principles about how we ought to live. It asks questions like: What are the basic principles of right and wrong? What things are ultimately worthwhile in life? What would a just society be like? What makes someone a good person? What are the basic human rights? Is abortion right or wrong?

Normative ethics has two levels. **Normative theory** looks for very general moral principles, like "We *ought* always to do whatever maximizes the total pleasure for everyone." **Applied normative ethics** studies moral questions about specific areas, like abortion or lying. Both levels formulate and defend moral principles. They say things like "We *ought* to do such and such ..."

Metaethics is the more basic branch of moral philosophy, since it studies the method for selecting moral principles and doing normative ethics. So we'll start with metaethics. We'll first talk about method, and then later use this method to arrive at principles about how we ought to live. Our remaining chapters divide into four groups:

- Chapters 1 to 3 consider three views popular among ordinary people: that morality is based on social conventions, personal feelings, or God's will.
- Chapters 4 to 6 consider three views popular among philosophers: that morality is based on self-evident truths, emotional exclamations, or rational imperatives.
- Chapters 7 to 9 give a practical approach to moral rationality that stresses consistency and the golden rule.
- Chapters 10 to 12 are about normative ethics – and thus discuss principles about how we ought to live.

Chapter 12 is a "synthesis chapter." It tries to unify our understanding of the views in this book, and what difference they make, by applying them to the hotly disputed topic of abortion.

D.   Why study ethics?

I can think of three reasons to study moral philosophy – besides the fact that, for many of us, it's very interesting.

First, moral philosophy can deepen our reflection on the ultimate questions of life. This is of value in itself, regardless of its practical benefits. If you haven't wrestled with some of life's deeper questions, then you aren't a well-educated person.

Second, moral philosophy can help us to think better about morality. As we make moral judgments, we implicitly assume an approach to morality, or perhaps a confused mixture of approaches. Our approach, whether good or bad, whether defensible or not, gives us a perspective for thinking and acting. Moral philosophy can improve our perspective, and make it more reflective and better thought out. And it can improve our thinking about specific moral issues.

As we grow up, we're continually told what is good or bad, or what we ought or ought not to do. Our parents tell us this – as do our teachers, our friends, and the wider society. Eventually, we have to sort through these values and form our own beliefs. But how can we do this in the wisest and best way? That's the central issue of moral philosophy.

A third goal of moral philosophy is to sharpen our general thinking processes. When we do philosophy, we learn important intellectual skills. We learn to think rigorously about fundamental questions – to understand and evaluate conflicting points of view – to express ideas clearly – and to reason in a careful way. These skills are valuable in real life, and philosophy can help develop them like nothing else can.

E. Study suggestions

You'll learn better if you grasp the structure of the chapters:

- Each chapter begins with a title page, and then one or two introductory paragraphs. These give you an overview.
- Important terms are introduced in **bold type**. Learn each term and be able to give a definition. The Glossary at the end of the book has a collection of definitions.
- A chapter summary helps you review what you've read.
- Study questions ask about key ideas. Write out the answers and keep them in an "ethics folder." Your teacher may want to collect these, to check your work and make suggestions.
- The last section of each chapter talks about computer exercises, Internet Web resources, and further readings.

You'll find that the study questions and computer exercises are very useful tools to help you to learn the material.

Most chapters begin with a presentation by a fictional student. In the next chapter, you'll listen to the fictional "Ima Relativist" explain and defend cultural relativism. Take her view seriously and try to understand it. Make sure that you can explain it without distorting it or using slanted language. A good motto for doing philosophy is "Understand before you criticize." After you understand the view, reflect on how plausible you find it and how well it accords with your own thinking. Then look for problems and objections.

Read the fictional presentation several times, from various perspectives. First read to get the general idea. Read it again to get the details; be sympathetic, as if you were listening to a friend explain her views. Read it again in a critical way; try to uncover weak points and objections.

Finally, after you've discussed the view in class, read it again to see where you stand.

After each fictional presentation, I'll bring up objections. Consider these carefully, and try to formulate them in your own words. Then ask yourself whether they are good objections, or whether they misunderstand the view or can be answered. Perhaps you have further objections yourself.

Practically every view, even a false one, can teach us something. If you reject a view, you may still want to incorporate some of its ideas into your own thinking. Or you may want to use the rejected view to help you to develop a sharply opposed perspective.

Relate the views to practical issues. Ask how a view would help you to argue against racist actions – or how it would lead you to teach morality to your children. Concrete applications can help us to understand philosophical views and see their practical relevance.

This book is an introduction to moral philosophy and isn't meant to be the last word on the subject. There's much more to say about all of this; a more advanced book would be much more complicated. The end of each chapter mentions further readings, in case you want to pursue matters further.

Moral philosophy is difficult and controversial. As you study it, you may at times feel perplexed and overwhelmed; this is a normal reaction. Radically opposed views can seem equally plausible, and a view that seems convincing at first can sometimes be demolished by a few well-placed objections. Don't be discouraged; instead, try to make progress. You may not arrive at the final answers, but you can hope to improve your understanding of morality and to arrive at answers that are more adequate and better thought out.

F.   Chapter summary

To do philosophy is to reason about the ultimate questions of life – questions like "Is there a God?" and "Are our actions free or determined?"

Philosophy reasons about such questions. We first try to get clear on what the question is asking. Then we consider the range of possible answers. We criticize each answer as brutally as we can; and we eliminate views that lead to absurdities. We look for the most adequate of the remaining views. If we can't completely resolve the issue, at least we can hope to arrive at a well thought-out view.

Reasoning about philosophical questions involves constructing arguments, which consist in premises and a conclusion. We aim for clearly true premises from which our conclusion logically follows. The most common way to reason is to attack a view by showing that it logically implies things that are false or doubtful.

To do moral philosophy is to reason about the ultimate questions of morality. Moral philosophy has two parts:

- Metaethics studies the nature and methodology of moral judgments. It deals with what "good" means, whether there are moral truths, and how we can justify or rationally defend beliefs about right and wrong.

- Normative ethics studies principles about how we ought to live. It looks for norms about what is right or wrong, worthwhile, virtuous, or just.

Metaethics is more basic, since it studies the method for selecting moral principles and doing normative ethics.

In this book we'll first consider various views about the nature and methodology of ethics. Then we'll consider a practical approach to moral rationality that stresses consistency and the golden rule. Then we'll deal with some issues of normative ethics.

In studying moral philosophy, we'll be wrestling with some of the great questions of life, refining our thinking about morality, and sharpening our general thinking processes.

G.   Study questions

Write out the answers in your ethics folder. If you don't know an answer, go back to the section that deals with it.

1.   What is philosophy? Give two examples of questions that philosophy deals with. (A)
2.   If you had a previous philosophy course, what explanation or definition of "philosophy" did you learn? Give two philosophical issues that you dealt with.
3.   What other subjects deal with ultimate questions? How does their approach differ from that of philosophy?
4.   Philosophy *reasons* about ultimate questions. Explain what this "reasoning" in a general sense involves. (B)

5. What is logical reasoning? What is an argument? What two things do we need to do to prove something?
6. What is the most common way to argue against a philosophical view?
7. What is moral philosophy? (C)
8. Explain the two basic questions of moral philosophy – and the difference between metaethics and normative ethics.
9. Why should we study moral philosophy? (D)
10. Who is Ima Relativist and how should we approach her view? (E)

H. For further study

To solidify your understanding, do the computer exercises for "Ethics 00 – Introduction." The Computer Exercises appendix at the end of this book has further information on this and on Internet resources.

For brief discussions of the nature of philosophy and of moral philosophy, see Passmore's "Philosophy" and Nielsen's "Problems of ethics." For a more thorough introduction to logic, see Chapter 1 of Gensler's *Logic: Analyzing and Appraising Arguments*.

You may at times wish to consult other introductory ethics texts and what they say about the various views. I suggest the brief *Ethics* by Frankena (my dissertation director) or the more detailed *Ethical Theory* by Brandt. The *Encyclopedia Britannica* has many useful articles on ethics (look under "Ethics: 20th-century Western ethics"), as do the *Encyclopedia of Philosophy* and the *Encyclopedia of Ethics*. There are many fine ethics anthologies, including Johnson's *Ethics: Selections from Classical and Contemporary Writers*. The Bibliography at the end of the book has information on how to find these works.

CHAPTER 1
Cultural Relativism

CHAPTER 1
Cultural Relativism

> **Cultural Relativism (CR):**
>
> "Good" means "socially approved."
>
> Pick out your moral principles by following what your society approves of.

Cultural relativism (CR) says that good and bad are relative to culture. What is "good" is what is "socially approved" in a given culture. Our moral principles describe social conventions and must be based on the norms of our society.

We'll begin by listening to the fictional Ima Relativist explain her belief in cultural relativism. As you read this and similar accounts, reflect on how plausible you find the view and how well it harmonizes with your own thinking. After listening to Ima, we'll consider various objections to CR.

1.1   Ima Relativist

My name is Ima Relativist. I've embraced cultural relativism as I've come to appreciate the deeply cultural basis for morality.

I was brought up to believe that morality is about objective facts. Just as snow is white, so also infanticide is wrong. But attitudes vary with time and place. The norms that I was taught are the norms of my own society; other societies have different ones. Morality is a cultural construct. Just as societies create different styles of food and clothing, so too they create different moral codes. I've learned about these in my anthropology class and experienced them as an exchange student in Mexico.

Consider my belief that infanticide is wrong. I was taught this as if it were an objective standard. But it isn't; it's just what my society holds. When I say "Infanticide is wrong," this just means that my society disapproves of it. For the ancient Romans, on the other hand, infanticide was all right. There's no sense in asking which side here is "correct." Their view is true relative to their culture, and our view is true relative to ours. There are no objective truths about right or wrong. When we claim otherwise, we're just imposing our culturally taught attitudes as the "objective truth."

"Wrong" is a relative term. Let me explain what this means. Something isn't "to the left" absolutely, but only "to the left *of*" this or that. Similarly, something isn't "wrong" absolutely, but only "wrong *in*" this or that society. Infanticide might be wrong in one society but right in another.

We can express CR most clearly as a definition: "X is good" means "The majority (of the society in question) approves of X." Other moral terms, like "bad" and "right," can be defined in a similar way. Note the reference to a specific society. Unless otherwise specified, the society in question is that of the person making the judgment. When I say "Hitler acted *wrongly*," I mean "according to the standards of *my* society."

The myth of objectivity says that things can be good or bad "absolutely" – not relative to this or that culture. But how can we know what is good or bad absolutely? How can we argue about this without just presupposing the standards of our own society? People who speak of good or bad absolutely are absolutizing the norms of their own society. They take the norms that they were taught to be objective facts. Such people need to study anthropology, or to live for a time in another culture.

As I've come to believe in cultural relativism, I've grown in my acceptance of other cultures. Like many exchange students, I used to have this "we're right and they're wrong" attitude. I struggled against this. I came to realize that the other side isn't "wrong" but just "different." We have to see others from their point of view; if we criticize them, we're just imposing the standards of our own society. We cultural relativists are more tolerant.

Through cultural relativism I've also come to be more accepting of the norms of my own society. CR gives a basis for a common morality within a culture – a democratic basis that pools everyone's ideas and insures that the norms have wide support. So I can feel solidarity with my own people, even though other groups have different values.

Before going to Section 1.2, reflect on your initial reaction to cultural relativism. What do you like or dislike about the view? Do you have any objections?

1.2   Objections to CR

Ima has given us a clear formulation of an approach that many find attractive. She's thought a lot about morality, and we can learn from her. Yet I'm convinced that her basic perspective on morality is wrong. Ima will likely come to agree as she gets clearer in her thinking.

Let me point out the biggest problem. CR forces us to conform to society's norms – or else we contradict ourselves. If "good" and "socially approved" meant the same thing, then whatever was one would have to be the other. So this reasoning would be valid:

> Such and such is socially approved.
> ∴ Such and such is good.

If CR were true, then we couldn't consistently disagree with the values of our society. But this is an absurd result. We surely can consistently disagree with the values of our society. We can consistently affirm that something is "socially approved" but deny that it is "good." This would be impossible if CR were true.

Ima could **bite the bullet** (accept the implausible consequence), and say that it *is* self-contradictory to disagree morally with the majority. But this would be a difficult bullet for her to bite. She'd have to hold that civil rights leaders contradicted themselves when they disagreed with accepted views on segregation. And she'd have to accept the majority view on all moral issues – even if she sees that the majority is ignorant.

Suppose that Ima learned that most people in her society approve of displaying intolerance and ridicule toward people of other cultures. She'd then have to conclude that such intolerance is good (even though this goes against her new insights):

> Intolerance is socially approved.
> ∴ Intolerance is good.

She'd have to either accept the conclusion (that intolerance is good) or else reject cultural relativism. Consistency would require that she change at least one of her views.

Here's a bigger bullet for Ima to bite. Imagine that Ima meets a figure skater named Lika Rebel, who is on tour from a Nazi country. In Lika's homeland, Jews and critics of the government are put in concentration camps. The majority of the people, since they are kept misinformed, support these policies. Lika dissents. She says that these policies are supported by the majority but are wrong. If Ima applied CR to this case, she'd have to say something like this to Lika:

> Lika, your word "good" refers to what is approved in your culture. Since your culture approves of racism and oppression, you must accept that these are good. You can't think otherwise. The minority view is always wrong – since what is "good" is by definition what the majority approves.

CR is intolerant toward minority views (which are automatically wrong) and would force Lika to accept racism and oppression as good. These results follow from CR's definition of "good" as "socially approved." Once Ima sees these results, she'll likely give up CR.

Racism is a good test case for ethical views. A satisfying view should give some way to attack racist actions. CR fails at this, since it holds that racist actions are good in a society if they're socially approved. If Lika followed CR, she'd have to agree with a racist majority, even if they're misinformed and ignorant. CR is very unsatisfying here.

Moral education gives another test case for ethical views. If we accepted CR, how would we bring up our children to think about morality? We'd teach them to think and live by the norms of their society – whatever these were. We'd teach conformity. We'd teach that these are examples of correct reasoning:

- "My society approves of A, so A is good."
- "My peer-group society approves of getting drunk on Friday night and then driving home, so this is good."
- "My Nazi society approves of racism, so racism is good."

CR would make us uncritical about the norms of our society. These norms can't be in error – even if they come from stupidity and ignorance. Likewise, the norms of another society (even Lika's Nazi homeland) can't be in error or be criticized. Thus CR goes against the critical spirit that characterizes philosophy.

1.3   Moral diversity

CR sees the world as neatly divided into distinct societies. Each one has little or no moral disagreement, since the majority view determines what is right or wrong in that society. But the world isn't like that. Instead, the world is a confusing mixture of overlapping societies and groups; and individuals don't necessarily follow the majority view.

CR ignores the subgroup problem. We all belong to overlapping groups. I'm part of a specific nation, state, city, and neighborhood. And I'm also part of various family, professional, religious, and peer groups.

These groups often have conflicting values. According to CR, when I say "Racism is wrong" I mean "My society disapproves of racism." But *which* society does this refer to? Maybe most in my national and religious societies disapprove of racism, while most in my professional and family societies approve of it. CR could give us clear guidance only if we belonged to just one society. But the world is more complicated than that. We're all multicultural to some extent.

CR doesn't try to establish common norms *between* societies. As technology shrinks the planet, moral disputes between societies become more important. Nation A approves of equal rights for women (or for other races or religions), but nation B disapproves. What is a multinational corporation that works in both societies to do? Or societies A and B have value conflicts that lead to war. Since CR helps very little with such problems, it gives a poor basis for life in the twenty-first century.

How do we respond to moral diversity between societies? Ima rejects the dogmatic "we're right and they're wrong" attitude. And she stresses the need to understand the other side from their point of view. These are positive ideas. But Ima then says that neither side can be wrong. This limits our ability to learn. If our society can't be wrong, then it can't learn from its mistakes. Understanding the norms of another culture can't then help us to correct errors in our own norms.

Those who believe in objective values see the matter differently. They might say something like this:

> There's a truth to be found in moral matters, but no culture has a monopoly on this truth. Different cultures need to learn from each other. To see the errors and blind spots in our own values, we need to see how other cultures do things, and how they react to what we do. Learning about other cultures can help us to correct our cultural biases and move closer to the truth about how we ought to live.

1.4 Objective values

We need to talk more about the objectivity of values. This is a large and important topic, and we'll often return to it in later chapters.

The **objective view** (also called **moral realism**) claims that some things are objectively right or wrong, independently of what anyone may think or feel. Dr Martin Luther King, for example, claimed that racist actions were objectively wrong. The wrongness of racism was a fact. Any person or culture that approved of racism was mistaken. In saying this, King wasn't absolutizing the norms of his society; instead, he disagreed with accepted norms. He appealed to a higher truth about right and wrong, one that didn't depend on human thinking or feeling. He appealed to objective values.

Ima rejects this belief in objective values and calls it "the myth of objectivity." On her view, things are good or bad only relative to this or that culture. Things aren't good or bad objectively, as King thought. But are objective values really a "myth"? Let's examine Ima's reasoning.

Ima had three arguments against objective values. There can't be objective moral truths, she thought, because

1. morality is a product of culture,
2. cultures disagree widely about morality, and
3. there's no clear way to resolve moral differences.

But these arguments fall apart if we examine them carefully.

(1) "Since morality is a product of culture, there can't be objective moral truths." The problem with this reasoning is that a product of culture can express objective truths. Every book is a product of culture; and yet many books express objective truths. So too, a moral code could be a product of culture and yet still express objective truths about how people ought to live.

(2) "Since cultures disagree widely about morality, there can't be objective moral truths." But the mere fact of disagreement doesn't show that there's no truth of the matter, that neither side is right or wrong. Cultures disagree widely about anthropology or religion or even physics. Yet there may still be a truth of the matter about these subjects. So a wide disagreement on moral issues wouldn't show that there's no truth of the matter on moral issues.

We might also question whether cultures differ so deeply about morality. Most cultures have fairly similar norms against killing, stealing, and lying. Many moral differences can be explained as the application of similar basic values to differing situations. The golden rule, "Treat others as you want to be treated," is almost universally accepted across the world. And the diverse cultures that make up the United Nations have agreed to an extensive statement on basic human rights.

(3) "Since there's no clear way to resolve moral differences, there can't be objective moral truths." But there may be clear ways to resolve at least many moral differences. We need a way to reason about ethics that would appeal to intelligent and open-minded people of all cultures – and that would do for ethics what scientific method does for science. We'll work on this later, in Chapters 7 to 9.

Even if there were no solid way to know moral truths, it wouldn't follow that there are no such truths. There may be truths that we have no solid way of knowing about. Did it rain on this spot 500 years ago today? There's some truth about this, but we'll never know it. Only a small percentage of all truths are knowable. So there could be objective moral truths, even if we had no solid way to know them.

So Ima's attack on objective values fails. But this isn't the end of the matter, for there are further arguments on the issue. The dispute over objective values is important, and we'll talk more about it later. But before leaving this section, let me clarify some related points.

The objective view says that *some* things are objectively right or wrong, independently of what anyone may think or feel; but it still could accept much relativity in other areas. Many social rules clearly are determined by local standards:

- Local law: "Right turns on a red light are forbidden."
- Local rule of etiquette: "Use the fork only in your left hand."

We need to respect such local rules; otherwise, we may hurt people, either by crashing their cars or by hurting their feelings. On the objective view, the demand that we not hurt people is a rule of a different sort – a *moral* rule – and *not* determined by local customs. Moral rules are seen as more authoritative and objective than government laws or rules of etiquette; they are rules that *any* society must follow if it is to survive and prosper. If we go to a place where local standards permit hurting people for trivial reasons, then the local standards are mistaken. Cultural relativists would dispute this. They insist that local standards determine even basic moral principles; so hurting others for trivial reasons would be good if it were socially approved.

Respecting a range of cultural differences doesn't make you a cultural relativist. What makes you a cultural relativist is the claim that *anything* that is socially approved must thereby be good.

1.5   Social science

The popular stereotype says that all social scientists are cultural relativists. This is a false stereotype. Social scientists in fact hold a wide range of views on the foundations of ethics. Many reject CR. For example, the moral psychologist Lawrence Kohlberg saw CR as a relatively immature approach to morality, typical of teenagers and young adults.

Kohlberg claimed that we all, regardless of our culture, develop in our moral thinking through a series of stages. The first four go as follows:

1. Punishment/obedience: "bad" is what brings punishment.
2. Rewards: "good" is what brings you what you want.
3. Parental approval: "good" is what pleases Mommy and Daddy.
4. Social approval: "good" is what is socially approved.

Young children first think of morality in terms of punishment and obedience. Later they think more of rewards, and then parental approval. Still later, often in the teenage or early adult years, comes the CR stage. Here "good" is what is socially approved, first by the peer group, and then later by the larger society. Here it's important to wear the right kind of clothes and listen to the right kind of music – where the "right kind" is whatever is socially approved. Many beginning college students struggle with these issues. This may be why they take CR so seriously – even though the view is implausible when we study it carefully.

What comes after cultural relativism, according to Kohlberg? Sometimes confusion and skepticism follow; indeed, an ethics course may promote these. Then we may move into stage 5 (which resembles the rule utilitarian view of Chapter 10) or stage 6 (which resembles the golden-rule consistency view of Chapters 7 to 9). Both stages try to evaluate conventional norms rationally.

I don't bring up Kohlberg to argue that, since his descriptive account is correct, hence CR is wrong. His account is controversial. Many psychologists propose a different sequence of moral stages or reject the idea of stages. And we've adequately demolished CR; we don't need help from psychology. I mention Kohlberg, rather, because many people are pressured into accepting CR by the myth that all social scientists accept CR. But there's no such consensus. Kohlberg and many other social scientists emphatically reject CR. They see it as an immature stage of moral thinking in which we just conform to society.

Kohlberg's approach raises a problem about the meaning of "good." People may mean different things at different stages; a young child by "good" may mean "what pleases Mommy and Daddy." So we should see our quest in terms of what morally mature people mean by "good." If our argument is correct, morally mature people by "good" don't mean "socially approved."

1.6 Chapter summary

Cultural relativism holds that "good" means what is "socially approved" by the majority in a given culture. Infanticide, for example, isn't good or bad objectively; rather it's good in a society that approves of it, but bad in one that disapproves of it.

Cultural relativists see morality as a product of culture. They think that societies disagree widely about morality, and that we have no clear way to resolve the differences. They conclude that there are no objective values. Cultural relativists view themselves as tolerant; they see other cultures, not as "wrong," but as "different."

Despite its initial plausibility, CR has many problems. For example, CR makes it impossible to disagree with the values of our society. We all at times want to say that something is socially approved but not good. But this is self-contradictory if CR is true.

In addition, CR entails that intolerance and racism would be good if society approved of them. And it leads us to accept the norms of our society in an uncritical way.

Cultural relativism attacks the idea of objective values. But these attacks fall apart if we examine them carefully.

Many social scientists oppose CR. The psychologist Lawrence Kohlberg, for example, claimed that people of all cultures go through the same stages of moral thinking. CR represents a relatively low stage in which we simply conform to society. At more advanced stages, we reject CR; we become critical of accepted norms and think for ourselves about moral issues. How to do that is the topic of this book.

1.7   Study questions

Write out the answers in your ethics folder. If you don't know an answer, go back to the section that deals with it.

1. How does cultural relativism define "good"? What method does it follow for arriving at moral beliefs?
2. Ima grew up believing in objective values. What two experiences led her to embrace cultural relativism? (1.1)
3. When Ima rejected "objective values" or "the myth of objectivity," what exactly did she reject? What does it mean to say that "good" is a relative term?
4. Why does cultural relativism supposedly make us more tolerant of other cultures?
5. What benefits does CR supposedly have for Ima's society?
6. Write about a page sketching your initial reaction to cultural relativism. Does it seem plausible to you? What do you like and dislike about it? Can you think of any way to show that it's false?

7. Why does CR make us conform to society's values? Does CR seem plausible here? (1.2)
8. According to CR, what does "Tolerance is good" mean? Why doesn't CR necessarily imply that tolerance is good?
9. Explain the story about "Lika Rebel" – and how it presents a problem for Ima's approach.
10. How does CR apply to racism and to moral education?
11. Explain the subgroup problem. (1.3)
12. Can CR establish common norms between societies?
13. Sketch how a cultural relativist and a believer in objective values would answer this question: "Can learning about other cultures help us to correct errors in the values of our own culture?"
14. What was Dr Martin Luther King's view about objective values? How did it differ from Ima's? (1.4)
15. Explain and criticize Ima's three arguments for rejecting objective values.
16. On the objective view, how do basic moral rules differ from rules of law and etiquette?
17. Are all social scientists cultural relativists? How did the psychologist Kohlberg view cultural relativism? (1.5)
18. Sketch Kohlberg's stages of moral development.

1.8   For further study

To solidify your understanding, do the computer exercises for "Ethics 01 – Cultural Relativism." The Computer Exercises appendix at the end of this book has further information on this and on Internet resources.

Be careful of terminology if you do outside reading; what we call "cultural relativism" is sometimes called "ethical relativism." To sort out the different types of "relativism" in ethics, see Brandt's "Ethical relativism." For defenses of cultural relativism by prominent anthropologists, see Benedict's brief "A defense of cultural relativism" or Sumner's longer *Folkways*. Section 1.4 raised the problem of how to distinguish morality from other action guides, such as law and etiquette, which also say how we *ought* to live; Frankena's "Two concepts of morality" discusses this further. For Kohlberg's approach, see his brief "A cognitive-developmental approach to moral education" or his longer *Essays on Moral Development*. The Bibliography at the end of the book has information on how to find these works.

CHAPTER 2
Subjectivism

CHAPTER 2
Subjectivism

> **Subjectivism (SB):**
>
> "X is good" means "I like X."
>
> Pick out your moral principles
> by following your feelings.

Subjectivism (SB) says that moral judgments describe how we feel. To call something "good" is to say that we have a positive feeling toward it. The ideal observer view is a further refinement; it says that moral judgments describe how we'd feel if we were fully rational.

In this chapter, we'll listen to two fictional roommates, both named "Ima," and both different from Ima Relativist of the previous chapter. Ima Subjectivist will defend subjectivism, and Ima Idealist will defend the ideal observer view. We'll also consider objections to the two views.

2.1   Ima Subjectivist

My name is Ima Subjectivist; but since my roommate is also named "Ima," I usually go by the name "Sub." I've embraced subjectivism as I've come to see that morality is deeply emotional and personal.

I took an anthropology course last year with some friends. We all came to believe in cultural relativism (CR) – the view that good and bad are relative to culture, that "good" means "socially approved." Later I saw a big problem with CR, namely that it denies us the freedom to form our own moral judgments. Moral freedom is very important to me.

CR would force me to accept all of society's values. Suppose that I found out that most people approve of racist actions; then I'd have to conclude that such actions are good. I'd contradict myself if I said "Racism is socially approved but not good." Since CR imposes the answers from the outside, and denies my freedom to think for myself on moral issues, I find the view repulsive.

Growing up requires that we question our inherited values. Yes, we do get our values from society, at least initially. As children, we get values mostly through our parents and peer groups. But then we grow into adulthood. As we do so, we question the values that we've learned. We might accept these values, or we might reject them, or we might partly accept them and partly reject them. The choice is up to us.

When I say "This is good," I'm talking about my own feelings – I'm saying "I like this." My value judgments are about how I feel, not about how society feels. My value judgments describe my own emotions.

I see moral freedom as part of the process of growing up. We expect children to parrot the values that they were taught; but adults who do this are stunted in their growth. We expect adults to think things out and form their own values. CR doesn't let us do this. Instead, it makes us conform to society.

Let me give an example of how subjectivism works. My family taught me a strict prohibition against drinking. In my family, any drinking was "socially prohibited." But my college friends think that it's cool to drink heavily. In this group, heavy drinking is "socially demanded." CR tells me that I must do what my society tells me – but which society? Should I follow my family, or my college friends?

SB tells me to follow my feelings. So I sat down and thought about the conflicting norms and the reasons behind them. My family wanted to guard against the excesses of drinking, while my friends used drinking to promote fun and sociability. I have positive feelings about both goals, and I thought about how best to promote them. After reflection, my feelings became clear. My feelings said to drink moderately.

Heavy drinking may be "cool" (socially approved), but it often leads to fights, hangovers, alcoholism, unwanted pregnancies, and traffic deaths. I don't like these consequences – and so I'm emotionally against heavy drinking. I say that it's bad. Many of my friends drink too much because this is socially approved. They behave like children. They blindly follow group values instead of thinking things out for themselves.

Let me explain some further points about SB. I said that "X is good" means "I *like* X." Some subjectivists prefer another emotional term – such as "feel positively about," "feel approval toward," or "desire." I won't worry about which term is the most accurate.

The truth of SB is obvious from how we speak. We often say things like "I like it – it's good." The two phrases mean the same thing. And we ask "Do you like it? – Do you think it's good?" Both ask the same question, but in different words.

My roommate objects that we can say that we like things that aren't good. For example, I say "I like smoking but it isn't good." But here I shift between evaluating the *immediate satisfaction* and evaluating the *consequences*. It would be clearer to say, "I like the immediate satisfaction that I get from smoking (= the immediate satisfaction is good); but I don't like the consequences (= the consequences aren't good)."

SB holds that moral truths are relative to the individual. If I like X but you don't, then "X is good" is true for me but false for you. We use "good" to talk about our positive feelings. Nothing is good or bad in itself, apart from our feelings. Values exist only in the preferences of individual people. You have your preferences and I have mine; no preference is objectively correct or incorrect. Believing this has made me more tolerant toward those who have different feelings and thus different moral beliefs.

My roommate protests that moral judgments make an objective claim about what is true in itself, apart from our feelings, and that subjectivism leaves this out. But objectivity is an illusion that comes because we objectify our subjective reactions. We laugh at a joke and call it "funny" – as if funniness were an objective property of things. We have a feeling of strangeness about something and call it "weird" – as if weirdness were an objective property. Similarly, we like something and call it "good" – as if goodness were an objective property of the thing. We subjectivists aren't fooled by this grammatical illusion.

In practice, everyone follows their feelings in moral matters. But only we subjectivists are honest enough to admit this and avoid the pretense of objectivity.

Before going to Section 2.2, reflect on your initial reaction to subjectivism. What do you like or dislike about the view? Do you have any objections?

2.2 Objections to SB

Sub (Ima Subjectivist) has given us a clear formulation of an important approach to morality. I agree with his stress on moral freedom and his rejection of cultural relativism (and of any other view that denies our moral freedom). But I disagree with his analysis of "good." And I think that he needs to develop his thinking about moral rationality.

The biggest problem is that subjectivism makes goodness depend completely on what we like. If "X is good" and "I like X" mean the same thing, then this reasoning is valid:

I like X.
∴ X is good.

Suppose that Sub's irresponsible friends like to get drunk and hurt people. Then they can deduce that such actions are good:

I like getting drunk and hurting people.
∴ Getting drunk and hurting people is good.

But this reasoning isn't correct: the conclusion doesn't follow. SB gives a very crude approach to morality, whereby we simply do as we like.

Even worse, my likes and dislikes would *make* things good or bad. Suppose that I like to hurt people; that would *make* it good to hurt people. Or suppose that I like to flunk students just for fun; that would *make* it good to flunk students just for fun. Whatever I like would thereby become good – even if my liking came from stupidity and ignorance.

Racism is a good test case for ethical views. SB is unsatisfying here, since it says that hurting other races is good if I like to do it. And SB implies that Hitler spoke the truth when he said "The killing of Jews is good" (since his statement just meant that he liked the killing of Jews). So SB has bizarre implications about racism.

Moral education gives another test case. If we accepted SB, how would we bring up our children to think about morality? We'd teach them to follow their feelings, to go by their likes and dislikes; but we'd give them no guidance on how to develop wise and responsible feelings. We'd teach children that "I like hurting people – therefore hurting people is good" is correct reasoning. So SB has bizarre implications about moral education.

So it's easy to poke holes in subjectivism. Why then does the view seem so plausible? One reason is that what we *like* tends to correspond with what we *think good*. SB explains this: calling something "good" just means that we like it. But other explanations are possible. Maybe we're motivated to like what our minds discover (perhaps through reason or religion) to be good. So other views too can explain the close connection between what we like and what we think good.

If we're morally immature, as we often are, the correspondence may fail. We may like things that we think bad, such as hurting other people. Morality is supposed to constrain our likes and dislikes. The thought that hurting others is bad can keep us from doing it, although we'd like to do it. So we can't identify what is good with what we like – even though the two would correspond closely if we were morally mature.

Not many philosophers today hold subjectivism. Some who have SB tendencies have moved to **emotivism**, which differs in a subtle way. These two views interpret "good" as follows:

- Subjectivism: "X is good" means "I like X."
- Emotivism: "X is good" means "Hurrah for X!"

Emotivism (which we'll take in Chapter 5) says that moral judgments are emotional exclamations and not truth claims; this is much like SB, but harder to refute. Others with SB tendencies have moved to the ideal observer view, which takes "good" to refer, not to our actual feelings, but to how we'd feel if we were fully rational; this approach combines reason and feeling. We'll hear about this view in the next section.

Sub talked about our freedom to form our own moral beliefs. But he didn't say how to use this freedom in a responsible way. He said we need to follow our feelings. But he didn't say how to develop wise feelings. Our next view tries to deal with these deficiencies by bringing in a richer view of moral rationality.

Ideal Observer View (IO):

"X is good" means "We'd desire X if we were fully informed and had impartial concern for everyone."

Pick out your moral principles by trying to become as informed and impartial as possible – and then seeing what you desire.

2.3   Ima Idealist

My name is Ima Idealist. I've embraced the ideal observer view as I've come to see the need to combine feelings with reason in our moral thinking.

Feelings and reason are both part of life; ideally, they should work together in everything we do. Take the example of grammar. Before I turn in an essay, I read it over looking for grammatical errors. My feelings alert me to such errors; when a sentence causes me distress, that tips me off that it may be ungrammatical. Of course, my feelings about grammar have been trained over the years by reason – by rules and examples. So my sense of grammar combines feelings with reason. Every aspect of life should combine these two.

You might know my roommate, Ima Subjectivist. Since we both have the same first name, which gets confusing, I just call him "Sub." Now Sub has some fine ideas, but they lack balance. He preaches "Follow your feelings" all the time. Now his advice isn't bad if you have wise and rational feelings. But his advice is *very* bad if your feelings are foolish.

I followed Sub's advice last semester, and it led to problems. I followed my feelings about eating – and I gained fifty pounds. I followed my feelings about when to attend class – and I nearly flunked out of school. I insulted people when I felt like doing so – and I alienated myself from others. Now I don't like what I did. In retaliation against Sub for his bad advice, I put this sign on our wall:

> If we just do as we like, we soon won't like what we've made of our lives.

We often need to train our feelings, instead of just following them blindly. For example, I used to like smoking, overeating, and insulting people. But I saw that these weren't good things to like – and so eventually I came to dislike them.

We need to combine feelings with rationality. My motto now is "Develop rational moral feelings first – and then follow your feelings." But how, you may ask, do we develop rational moral feelings? I have two suggestions:

1. *Be informed:* Base your feelings and decisions on a correct assessment of the situation.
2. *Be impartial:* Make your moral judgments from an impartial standpoint that shows concern for everyone.

Rational moral feelings are feelings that are informed and impartial.

Moral judgments don't describe our actual feelings, our momentary impulses, what we happen to like at the moment. Instead, moral judgments describe how we'd feel if we were fully rational in our feelings. "X is good" means "We'd desire X if we were fully informed and impartial." This approach is called the **ideal observer view**. On this approach, we pick out our moral principles by trying to be as informed and impartial as possible – and then seeing how we feel.

My friend Sub was puzzled that we can say "I *like* smoking but it isn't *good*." He had a convoluted explanation of why the statement makes sense. My explanation is better. "Liking" is about our actual feelings; "good" is about how we'd feel if we were rational. Here our pro-smoking impulses conflict with a rational perspective (which includes knowing and taking account of the harmful consequences of smoking).

Let me explain my view in another way. An **ideal observer** is an imaginary person of supreme moral wisdom – a person who is fully informed and has impartial concern for everyone. To call something "good" means that we'd desire it if we were ideal observers. Of course, we'll never be ideal observers, since we'll always have some ignorance and bias. But the notion of an ideal observer is useful; it gives a vivid picture of moral wisdom and a way to understand the meaning and methodology of moral judgments.

Let me explain how to make moral judgments in a rational way. First, we need to be informed. We need to know about circumstances, alternatives, and consequences. We need to avoid factual errors. Our moral judgments are less rational if they aren't based on a correct understanding of the situation. Of course, we can't know everything; but we can strive for greater knowledge.

The second element of rational moral thinking is impartiality. Moral judgments involve *impartial* feelings. When we make moral judgments, we take an impartial perspective that shows concern for everyone. We need this perspective to regulate our selfish inclinations, so that we can all live together in peace and harmony.

Impartiality shows the errors in subjectivism further. On subjectivism, "X is good" means "I like X" – so this way of reasoning is correct:

I like getting drunk and hurting people.
∴ Getting drunk and hurting people is good.

But this reasoning is incorrect. The conclusion misuses "good," since this word describes what we'd desire if we were fully informed *and impartial*. The conclusion clearly doesn't show an impartial concern for everyone. Society would fall apart if everyone followed the subjectivist model of moral reasoning – where we just do what we like, regardless of how this affects other people.

Here's an example of how to apply my view. Suppose that you are elected to Congress. On what basis do you appraise a proposed law as "good," and thus as worthy of your vote? Cultural relativism tells you to go with what the majority favors; but the majority can be ignorant, or swayed by propaganda and lies. Subjectivism tells you to follow your feelings; but your feelings can be ignorant or biased. My view tells you to form your values in a way that is factually informed and impartially concerned for everyone. This would give a better basis for democracy.

My view gives objective ways to criticize racist moral beliefs. Suppose that we're evaluating the moral rationality of a Nazi who believes that he ought to put Jews in concentration camps. The Nazi likely violates our "Be informed" condition, because he likely bases his attitudes on factual errors or ignorance:

- His attitudes might be based on *factual errors*. Maybe he falsely believes that his own race is superior or racially pure. Or maybe he falsely believes that racist policies will greatly benefit his own race. We can objectively criticize such errors.

- His attitudes might be based on *ignorance*. Maybe he doesn't understand the suffering that his actions cause his victims. Or maybe he doesn't understand how diverse races in some other societies have learned to live together in peace and harmony. Or maybe he doesn't understand how his hatred of Jews came from indoctrination (including lies and false stereotypes).

We also could criticize his attitudes on the basis of *impartiality*. Since his actions don't show an impartial concern for everyone, it makes no sense for him to defend these actions using moral language. He might *like* to persecute Jews, but he can't plausibly hold that these actions are *good*.

On my approach, some value systems are more rational than others. A system of values is "rational" – and thus worthy of our respect – if it's based on a correct understanding of the facts and an impartial concern for everyone. Nazism, slavery, and apartheid are irrational – since they're based on ignorance or violations of impartial concern.

My view has several advantages over cultural relativism and subjectivism. It adds a rational element while also recognizing the role of feelings. It gives stronger ammunition for attacking racism. It provides a firmer basis for moral education, since it guides us on how to develop wise and responsible feelings. And it accords with how we form our moral beliefs when we try to be rational.

Before going to Section 2.4, reflect on your initial reaction to the ideal observer view. What do you like or dislike about it? Do you have any objections?

2.4   Objections to IO

The ideal observer view is a vast improvement over cultural relativism and subjectivism. But unfortunately the view, at least as we've developed it so far, still has problems.

The "impartiality" condition is unclear. Does it require that we have an equal concern for everyone, regardless of whether the person is our child or a complete stranger? Would this be a good thing? If impartiality doesn't require this, then what exactly does it require?

The condition to be "fully informed" seems too idealized. Wouldn't it require an infinite amount of knowledge, and thus an infinite brain? If humans are incapable of being fully informed, does it even make sense to ask what we'd desire if we were fully informed?

The view arbitrarily gives us just two rationality conditions. Are there others besides these two? For example, do we also need to be consistent? Do we also need to have empathy (a vivid awareness of what it would be like to be in another's place)? Some philosophers include these or other conditions. How do we decide which rationality conditions to include?

Ideal observers might disagree on some issues. If they disagree, then should we take "good" to be what "most" (not "all") ideal observers would desire? Or should we each follow what we as individuals would desire if we were ideal observers?

So the ideal observer view, while a huge step forward, is not yet the end of our journey. Its ideas need to be developed further. But any better view would likely need to build on its insights.

2.5   Chapter summary

Subjectivism says that our moral judgments describe our personal feelings: "X is good" means "I like X." We are to pick out our moral principles by following our feelings.

Subjectivism has problems. It holds, implausibly, that the mere fact that we like something (such as getting drunk and hurting others) would make it good. It gives a weak basis for dealing with practical areas like racism and moral education. And it tells us to follow our feelings but gives us no guide on how to develop rational and wise feelings.

The ideal observer view tries to combine feelings with rationality. It says that "X is good" means "We'd desire X if we were fully informed and had impartial concern for everyone." We are to pick out our moral principles by first trying to develop rational moral feelings (by striving to become informed and impartial) – and then following our feelings.

The ideal observer view, while a vast improvement over cultural relativism and subjectivism, still has problems, at least as we've developed the view so far. For example, it arbitrarily gives us just two rationality conditions – and it's unclear what "impartial" means.

2.6 Study questions

Write out the answers in your ethics folder. If you don't know an answer, go back to the section that deals with it.

1. How does subjectivism define "good"? What method does it follow for arriving at moral beliefs?
2. Sub (Ima Subjectivist) once believed in cultural relativism. Why did he convert to subjectivism? (2.1)
3. How did Sub relate moral freedom to the process of growing up?
4. How did Sub apply SB to the issue of drinking?
5. How is the truth of SB supposed to be obvious from how we speak?
6. Does SB see values as relative? What are they relative to?
7. How did Sub handle the objection that moral judgments make an objective claim about what is true in itself, apart from our feelings?
8. Write about a page sketching your initial reaction to subjectivism. Does it seem plausible to you? What do you like and dislike about it? Can you think of any way to show that it's false?
9. Give some objections to subjectivism. (2.2)
10. In actual fact, do our moral judgments necessarily correspond to our likes and dislikes?
11. How does SB apply to racism and moral education?
12. How does the ideal observer view define "good"? What method does it follow for arriving at moral beliefs? (2.3)
13. What was Ima Idealist's major objection to subjectivism?
14. How do we develop rational moral feelings? Explain the two rationality conditions.
15. What is an "ideal observer"? Do any ideal observers exist? If not, then what is the point of the idea?
16. How would we apply the ideal observer view if we were elected to Congress?
17. How does the ideal observer view apply to racism?
18. Write about a page sketching your initial reaction to the ideal observer view. Does it seem plausible to you? What do you like and dislike about it? Can you think of any way to show that it's false?
19. Sketch two problems with the ideal observer view. (2.4)

2.7 For further study

To solidify your understanding, do the computer exercises for "Ethics 02 – Subjectivism." The Computer Exercises appendix at the end of this book has further information on this and on Internet resources.

Hume's eighteenth-century *A Treatise of Human Nature* (especially Part 1 of Book 3) is the classic defense of subjectivism. Hume had further arguments for the view; for example, he argued that, since moral judgments influence our actions and feelings, they must be emotional and not just judgments of reason. His later *Enquiry Concerning the Principles of Morals* (especially Section 9 and Appendix 1) moved toward the ideal observer view. For more recent defenses of this view, see Firth's brief "Ethical absolutism and the ideal observer" or Carson's longer *The Status of Morality*. The Bibliography at the end of the book has information on how to find these works.

CHAPTER 3
Supernaturalism

CHAPTER 3

Supernaturalism

Supernaturalism (SN):

"X is good" means "God desires X."

Pick out your moral principles by following God's will.

Supernaturalism (SN) says that moral judgments describe God's will. Calling something "good" means that God desires it. Ethics is based on religion.

We'll begin by listening to the fictional Ima Supernaturalist explain her belief in supernaturalism. After considering some objections, we'll see how religion and ethics might connect even if SN is wrong.

3.1 Ima Supernaturalist

My name is Ima Supernaturalist. I've embraced supernaturalism as I've come to appreciate the deeply religious basis for morality.

In Sunday School, I learned that God gave us the ten commandments:

---

1. Thou shalt not worship false gods.
2. Thou shalt not take God's name in vain.
3. Keep holy the Sabbath.
4. Honor thy father and thy mother.
5. Thou shalt not kill.
6. Thou shalt not commit adultery.
7. Thou shalt not steal.
8. Thou shalt not bear false witness.
9. Thou shalt not covet thy neighbor's wife.
10. Thou shalt not covet thy neighbor's goods.

The ten commandments are from the Old Testament (Exodus 20 and Deuteronomy 5). They express God's will, and thus form the practical rules for morality. Jesus later taught that the deeper idea behind the commandments was to love God above all things and love our neighbor as ourselves (Matthew 22:37–40). He also summed up the commandments in the golden rule, which says "Treat others as you want to be treated" (Matthew 7:12).

I must admit that religion didn't mean much to me for many years. For a time, I was a "lost soul." I did drugs, and I stole money to support my drug habit. My life was going down the drain. But then I connected with a Christian group and had a religious conversion. Now God is a strong force in my life. To do the right thing is to follow his will. I believe this – and it helped me to get my life back in order.

In my ethics course last semester, we took three secular approaches to morality. The first two based ethics on social approval and on personal feelings. These were the same things that led me into my drug habit; so I can testify, based on personal experience, that these two views can lead us to ruin. My teacher proposed, instead, that we do whatever a perfectly rational "ideal observer" would want us to do. This view is fine, but only if we add that God is the perfectly rational "ideal observer." Otherwise, we're only appealing to a vague hypothetical construct.

My view, **supernaturalism**, sees moral judgments as religious statements: "X is good" means "God desires X."

What does "God" here mean? The usual definition is "the all-good, all-powerful, all-knowing Creator of the world." But this would make my definitions circular (since I'd use "God" to define "good," and then "good" to define "God"). It would also suggest that there are standards of goodness prior to God's will (instead of God's will creating the standards). So it's better to define "God" as simply "the all-powerful, all-knowing Creator of the world."

I have three arguments for my view. My first argument presumes belief in the Bible. Given this belief, supernaturalism has to be true – because the Bible teaches it. The Bible always uses "good" as interchangeable with "what God desires." And the account of God writing the ten commandments on stone tablets teaches SN in a vivid way.

My second argument presumes belief in God. If you believe in God, then you'll believe that all basic laws of every sort depend on God's will. But then all basic *moral* laws depend on God's will. So God created the moral order, and his will distinguishes right from wrong.

My third argument presumes belief in an objective morality. If you accept that objective moral duties bind you, then you must admit a source of this obligation. This source could only be a non-person, or you, or other individuals, or society, or God. But the non-religious alternatives won't work. The source of obligation can't be:

- *a non-person* – since these are inferior to persons, and thus can't impose obligations on persons;
- *you* – since then you could release yourself from any obligation at will, and so you wouldn't have binding obligations;
- *other individuals or society* – since these have no moral authority over us if they tell us to do what is wrong.

The only source of obligation that works is God. Thus belief in objective moral duties requires belief in God. This argument doesn't presume belief in God, but it might lead to this belief.

My three arguments presume, respectively, that you believe in the Bible, or in God, or in an objective morality. If you don't believe in any of these, then I can't argue with you. But you're going to have a difficult time living your life if you don't decide to believe in something!

How does believing in the divine origin of values influence my life? I see three main influences. First, I regard morality as objective, and so I take it very seriously. Racist actions, for example, are objectively wrong, since God forbids them. So the duty to oppose racism is serious. Many supernaturalists are prepared to die in defense of their moral beliefs. I can't see how you could take morality seriously if it were based only on personal feelings or social approval.

Second, I connect morality closely with religion. So I have a strong religious motivation to be moral, and I follow a religious approach to moral education. One of the problems with the world today is that people try to teach morality without teaching religion – which won't work. So people grow up without any firm values.

Finally, I see atheists as confused about morality. At first I was perplexed that some atheists accept morality and try to live moral lives. But someone explained to me that atheists first got their values from a religious source. They lost their religion but kept the values – even though the values make sense only on a religious basis. So atheists who accept morality are confused. Clearheaded atheists like Sartre reject morality, saying that everything is permissible if there is no God.

What are we supernaturalists like? My parish paper mentioned a survey where people described us. Some talked about us as "intolerant judgmental fundamentalists" who look for clear-cut answers from above instead of struggling with moral issues. Others described us as "deeply religious people" who see morality, not as a set of abstract truths, but as part of our personal relationship with a loving God.

You shouldn't overly generalize about us. Yes, some supernaturalists are judgmental – even though Jesus forbade this (see Matthew 7:1–5). But others see that, as sinners ourselves, we should avoid "casting the first stone" against another (see John 8:7). And yes, some have selfish motives, obeying God just to avoid punishment and gain reward. But others, responding in gratitude to God's love, strive for an unselfish love toward God and neighbor. Since the Bible has to be understandable to a wide range of people, it appeals to both higher and lower motives.

3.2 Knowing God's will

This is still Ima. I need another section to tell you how we can know God's will. I'm sorry, but my view is more complicated than just doing what is socially approved or doing what you like.

So how can we know God's will? Supernaturalists differ on this. Four popular views say we can know God's will through (1) the Bible, (2) the church, (3) prayer, or (4) reason. Another view says that we *can't* know God's will.

First, there's the Bible. I was brought up to believe that the Bible teaches clear-cut answers on all moral issues. But I've learned that there are many gray areas where people interpret the Bible differently.

My Bible professor had been a pacifist during the Vietnam War. He believed that it was wrong to kill a human for any reason, even self-defense. He took "Thou shalt not kill" and "Turn the other cheek" literally. But many of his friends thought it their duty to fight the "godless Communists." They quoted Biblical passages urging the Israelites to conquer their enemies. So which side is right? Should a follower of the Bible be a pacifist or a militarist? And how do we decide this? I believe that we need to understand individual passages in the light of the Bible's general message. People who try to do this may end up interpreting things differently. So the Bible leaves us with gray areas. And of course the Bible doesn't directly address many issues.

There's also the problem of which religion and bible to follow. I have Jewish, Islamic, and Mormon friends who use different bibles. But all the bibles have the same general message about God's will, that God wants us to have concern and love for each other, and to treat others as we want to be treated. The details vary, but the general message is the same.

Second, there's the church. Many see their church as a moral author-ity. Some think that their church teaches an unchanging and infallibly true moral system, and that we must accept everything that it says. But history shows that church teaching has evolved over the years and sometimes has blind spots that need correction. My church mostly recognizes this. And so I don't take my church as an infallible guide on right and wrong. Instead, I look at my church as I look at a wise teacher: I listen and try to learn – but in the end I may disagree on some details.

Third, there's prayer. Many pray to God for guidance, and then take their feelings as a sign of God's will. I do this myself. But there's a danger of confusing my likes and dislikes with God's will. We've all seen religious fanatics who think that God wants things that in fact are crazy and hateful. So we need input from the Bible and the church to help us to form our conscience.

Fourth, there's reason. Some follow their moral intuitions, which they see as implanted by God to help us to know his will. Others follow an ideal-observer method, where we try to become as God-like as possible (striving for knowledge and love) and then see what we desire; this gives us an idea of what God would desire. These approaches can be helpful, particularly if we add input from the Bible and the church.

A final view is that we can't know God's will at all, since God is mysteriously above our little minds. As Romans 11:34 asks, "Who has known the mind of the Lord?" I think there's some truth here, but it's horribly overstated. Surely we know *some* things about God's will, even though we can't be sure about all the details. I get angry with people who think they know all the details and won't listen to anyone else.

So how can we know God's will? We need to combine all four sources: the Bible, the church, prayer, and reason. Where the sources speak clearly and in unison, our belief is very solid. So it's clear that God wants us to have concern and love for each other, and to treat others as we want to be treated. It's also clear that God opposes killing, stealing, and lying – and racism (which violates "Love thy neighbor"). But there are gray areas, like pacifism. Here we have to follow our prayer and reason as best we can, while we gain insight from the Bible and the church. In these gray areas, we should be less confident of our beliefs and more tolerant of opposing views.

Let me sum up SN's attractions. SN is popular among ordinary people; so it's not a view that only a philosopher could love. It explains morality in a clear way. It makes morality objective; human values have to conform to a higher law. It can appeal to higher motives (unselfish love and gratitude to God) or to lower ones (punishments and rewards). And it makes morality part of our personal relationship with God.

Before going to Section 3.3, reflect on your initial reaction to supernaturalism. What do you like or dislike about the view? Do you have any objections?

3.3 Ethics and atheists

Ima has given us a clear formulation of an important approach to morality. As a religious person, I agree with much of what she says. But I don't think that ethics and religion connect as closely as she claims. I don't think that moral judgments require belief in God, or that "X is good" means "God desires X." One problem is that Ima's view makes it impossible for atheists to make positive moral judgments.

Imagine an atheist who says the following:

> Kindness is good, but there is no God.

If "X is good" meant "God desires X," then this claim would be self-contradictory (since it would mean "God desires kindness, but there is no God"). But it isn't self-contradictory. So "X is good" doesn't mean "God desires X." Or we might argue this way:

> If supernaturalism were true, then atheists couldn't consistently make positive moral judgments.
> But atheists can consistently make positive moral judgments.
> ∴ Supernaturalism isn't true.

My argument doesn't presume any alternative view about what "good" means. But it does presume that our atheist friends aren't contradicting themselves when they make positive moral judgments.

Ima thinks that atheists with moral beliefs *are* contradicting themselves. Their moral beliefs presume God's existence, which they reject. Her explanation of how atheists got their values makes this seem more believable: "Atheists first got their values from a religious source. They lost their religion but kept the values – even though the values make sense only on a religious basis." But not all atheists got their values from religion. Morality can grow up in societies of atheists who have never taken the existence of God seriously. It's difficult to believe that such atheists by "good" mean "desired by God."

It's also difficult to believe that our atheist friends use "good" this way. Imagine that you're discussing a moral issue with an atheist friend. In the middle of the discussion, you suggest that you both stop using "good" and in its place use "desired by God." Would this substitution change the discussion? It would probably *end* the discussion. The atheist surely doesn't use the two expressions as equivalent in meaning.

This suggests a somewhat different response to my argument. Ima might claim that believers and atheists mean different things by "good." Believers mean "desired by God," while atheists mean something else. On this response, atheists could make moral judgments even if they deny God's existence.

But this second response makes it difficult to see how believers and atheists can have fruitful moral discussions. If both sides mean something different by "good," then they can't really agree or disagree morally. If I say "This is good" (meaning "God desires this") and the atheist says "This is good" (meaning something else), then we aren't agreeing – other than verbally.

I can have fruitful moral discussions with people even if I know nothing about their religion. For the most part, the discussion will go the same way regardless of religious beliefs. So believers and atheists seem to mean the same thing by "good." But atheists surely don't use "good" to mean "desired by God." So, presumably, neither believers nor atheists mean this by "good."

So there are strong objections to SN – and we'll see further objections in the next section. From a practical standpoint too, it would be better not to base ethics on something as controversial as religion. But a sufficiently determined supernaturalist could bite the bullet and hold to SN despite these objections.

3.4 Socrates's question

Socrates, the first major philosopher of ancient Greece, was a religious person who tried to follow God's will. He saw ethics as closely connected with religion. But he rejected SN – largely on the basis of a penetrating question. I'll express his question in my own words.

Let's suppose that there is a God, and that he desires all good things. We can ask this question:

> Is a good thing good *because* God desires it?
> Or does God desire it *because* it is good?

Let's assume that kindness is good and that God desires it. Which is based on which? Is kindness good because God desires it? Or does God desire kindness because it's already good?

Socrates and most other people take the second alternative. God desires kindness *because* he knows that it's good. His desires don't make it good. Instead, he wouldn't desire it if it weren't already good. But then kindness is good prior to and independently of God's will. It would presumably be good even if there were no God. This alternative involves giving up SN.

SN must take the first alternative. Here kindness is good *because* God desires it. Kindness wouldn't be good if God didn't desire it. Prior to God's desires, kindness is neither good nor bad. This answer, while possible, seems to make ethics arbitrary.

Here's another example. Let's assume that hatred is bad, and that God forbids it. Is hatred bad because God forbids it (so that if he didn't forbid it then it wouldn't be bad)? Or does God forbid it because it's already bad? This second alternative is more plausible, but it involves giving up supernaturalism.

This point is subtle, but of central importance. If you don't get the point, I suggest that you reread the last few paragraphs a few times until the idea comes through.

It might surprise you, but relatively few Christian philosophers take a clear stand in favor of the SN alternative (that God's will *makes* things good or bad). William of Ockham of the late Middle Ages was the most famous defender of SN, and he was regarded as a heretic.

Suppose that we take the SN alternative (that God's will *makes* things good or bad). We might then ask, "What if God desired hatred; would hatred then be good?" Ockham would have shouted, "Yes – if God desired hatred then hatred would be good!" But this is implausible.

Imagine that an all-powerful and all-knowing being created a world and desired that its people hate each other. Would hatred then be good? Surely not! Such a creator would have an evil will. But then we can't say that "good" by definition is what the creator desires.

Some might respond that God, being loving, wouldn't desire hatred. The mere desires of a creator wouldn't make a thing good; but the desires of a *loving* creator do make things good. But then wouldn't the loving act be good regardless of whether the creator desired it? If so, then again we must reject SN.

3.5 SN arguments

Ima had three arguments for SN. Supernaturalism must be true, she thought, because

1. the Bible teaches it,
2. all basic laws of every sort depend on God's will, and
3. God is the only plausible source of objective moral duties.

But these arguments fall apart if we examine them carefully.

(1) "Supernaturalism must be true – because the Bible teaches it." The problem here (even if we assume that what the Bible teaches must be true) is that the Bible doesn't really teach SN. The Bible, properly understood, doesn't take a stand for or against SN.

Years ago, my Bible teacher cautioned me against using the Bible to answer questions that the Biblical authors didn't ask and that wouldn't have made immediate sense to them. The Biblical authors weren't concerned with Socrates's question. Nor would it have made immediate sense to them. Thus it seems illegitimate to use the Bible to prove SN.

The Bible teaches that we ought to obey God; but this is compatible with other approaches to ethics. Maybe we ought to obey God because his commands reflect a deeper knowledge of an independent moral order. On this non-SN view, stealing isn't bad because God forbids it; instead, God forbids it because it's already bad. This non-SN approach is consistent with the Bible; nothing in the Bible contradicts it. If so, then believing in the Bible doesn't require that we be supernaturalists.

(2) "Supernaturalism must be true – because all basic laws of every sort depend on God's will." The problem here (even if we assume that there is a God) is that it's doubtful that all basic laws depend on God's will. Is "x = x" true because of God's will – so it would have been false if God had willed otherwise? The law seems true of its very nature, and not true because God made it true. Maybe basic moral laws are the same. Maybe hatred is evil in itself, and not just evil because God made it so.

(3) "Supernaturalism must be true – because God is the only plausible source of objective moral duties." The problem here (even if we assume that there are objective moral duties) is that it's doubtful that such duties need a source. To say that they need a source assumes that "A ought to be done" means something of the form "X legislates A." But why accept this? Maybe basic moral truths (like the logical truth "x = x") are true in themselves, and not true because someone made them true. Then they wouldn't need a "source."

3.6 Ethics and religion

How do ethics and religion connect? SN connects them with a definition: "X is good" means "God desires X." But SN has problems, even from a religious standpoint. Most religious thinkers reject SN but still want a close connection between ethics and religion. Let me sketch one possible approach to this – an approach close to that of St. Thomas Aquinas (an important Christian philosopher of the Middle Ages).

On the proposed view, God is a supremely good being. Calling God "good" doesn't mean that he fulfills his own desires. Instead, it means that his life accords with inherent truths about goodness – for example, that love is good in itself and hatred is bad in itself.

This view sees our origin and purpose in moral and religious terms. God created us so that our minds can know the good and our wills can freely choose it. God intends that our moral struggles purify us and lead us toward our ultimate goal, which is eternal happiness with him. In contrast, the atheistic view says that humans sprang up in a universe that's ultimately indifferent to moral concerns – and that life has no ultimate moral purpose.

On this religious view, basic moral truths are true in themselves. Believers and atheists both can use their God-given reason to know these truths. But divine revelation about morality can be useful, since our minds are often clouded. And so God commands us, "Thou shalt not steal." His command doesn't *make* stealing wrong; rather, he commands us because stealing is *already* wrong. While reason can tell us that stealing is wrong, we also can learn this through the Bible, the church, or prayer. Atheists as well as believers can know moral truths; but believers have additional ways to arrive at the same truths.

Believers also have additional motives for doing the right thing. An important motive is gratitude to God and love for his creatures. Doing the right thing is thus linked to our personal relationship to God.

Believers and non-believers will mostly come to the same moral beliefs, for example that stealing is wrong. But there may be differences. Believers will recognize a duty to worship God while non-believers won't. And there may be differences about issues like mercy killing, based on differences in beliefs about the origin and destiny of our lives.

This proposed view links ethics and religion closely, but it doesn't base ethics totally on religion. Ethics could exist without religion, but it would be incomplete. My purpose here isn't to defend or attack this view, but only to present it as an alternative to supernaturalism that is plausible from a religious standpoint.

3.7 Chapter summary

Supernaturalism holds that moral judgments describe God's will: "X is good" means "God desires X." God's will creates the moral order. Ethics is based on religion.

SN is defended as a Biblical teaching, as a consequence of belief in God (who is the source of all basic laws), and as the only plausible source of objectively binding duties. We can best know God's will through combining four sources: the Bible, the church, prayer, and reason.

SN, despite being initially plausible (at least to religious people), has some deep problems. SN seems to make it impossible for atheists to make positive moral judgments – an implausible result. And Socrates's question raises further problems: "Is a good thing good *because* God desires it? Or does God desire it *because* it is good?"

The arguments for SN fail if we examine them carefully. The Bible doesn't teach SN; rather, it teaches that we ought to obey God – which might be accepted and defended on a non-SN basis. SN isn't a consequence of belief in God; basic moral principles might be like the logical truth "x = x," which is true in itself, and not true because God decided to make it true. Finally, there are ways of defending the objectivity of ethics that don't base ethics on God's will.

Some are led to SN because of their conviction that ethics connects closely to religion. But it's possible to connect the two closely, even without SN.

3.8 Study questions

Write out the answers in your ethics folder. If you don't know an answer, go back to the section that deals with it.

1. How does supernaturalism define "good"? What method does it follow for arriving at moral beliefs?
2. How did Ima sum up Biblical teaching about God's will? (3.1)
3. What did Ima think of the three secular approaches to ethics (cultural relativism, subjectivism, and the ideal observer view) that she studied in her ethics course?
4. How did Ima define "God"? How did she avoid the danger of circular definitions?
5. What were Ima's three arguments for accepting SN?
6. In what three ways did SN affect Ima's life?

7. Some think that supernaturalists are "intolerant judgmental fundamentalists." How did Ima respond to this charge?
8. What problems did Ima mention about taking the Bible as the sole source of our knowledge about God's will? (3.2)
9. What problems did she mention about taking the church as the sole source of our knowledge about God's will?
10. How did Ima say that we might know God's will by appealing to prayer or reason?
11. How did Ima think that we can best know God's will?
12. Write about a page sketching your initial reaction to supernaturalism. Does it seem plausible to you? What do you like and dislike about it? Can you think of any way to show that it's false?
13. Explain the argument against SN based on the fact that atheists can make positive moral judgments? How would Ima respond to the argument? (3.3)
14. What was Socrates's question about supernaturalism? Explain the two possible answers. (3.4)
15. Criticize Ima's three arguments for supernaturalism. (3.5)
16. The book sketches a non-SN view about how ethics and religion connect. On this view, how would believers and atheists differ on (a) our origin and purpose, (b) our knowledge of moral truths, and (c) our motivation for leading moral lives? (3.6)

3.9 For further study

To solidify your understanding, do the computer exercises for "Ethics 03 – Supernaturalism." Also do review exercises "Ethics 03r" and "Ethics 03v." The Computer Exercises appendix at the end of this book has further information on these and on Internet resources.

For a short discussion of Ockham's supernaturalist ethics, see pages xlviii–l of the introduction to *Philosophical Writings of William of Ockham*. For a contemporary defense of supernaturalism, see Quinn's *Divine Commands and Moral Requirements*. Socrates's question about supernaturalism is on page 10 of Plato's *Euthyphro* dialogue. Sartre (in his *Existentialism and Human Emotions*) and Mackie (in his *Ethics*) are atheists who seem to agree that an objective ethics is possible only if it's based on God's will. For St. Thomas Aquinas's view, see his *Treatise on Law*. The Bibliography at the end of the book has information on how to find these works.

CHAPTER 4
Intuitionism

CHAPTER 4
Intuitionism

> **Intuitionism:**
>
> "Good" is indefinable. There are objective moral truths.
>
> Pick out your moral principles by following your basic moral intuitions.

Intuitionism says that "good" is an indefinable notion. There are objective moral truths that don't depend on human thinking or feeling. And the basic truths of morality, like the basic truths of mathematics, are self-evident to a mature mind.

We'll begin by listening to the fictional Ima Intuitionist explain his belief in intuitionism. Then we'll consider objections.

4.1   Ima Intuitionist

My name is Ima Intuitionist. I've embraced intuitionism as I've come to see that morality is objective and that the basic moral truths are already present inside of us, in our own minds.

I'm a philosophy major and intend to go to law school. So I'm interested in ethics and reasoning. While I've read much philosophy, I've also found much wisdom in the simple truths of common sense.

My favorite philosophers are the early twentieth-century British thinkers, G.E. Moore and W.D. Ross. They explained and defended commonsense morality. Their view, and mine, is called **intuitionism**. It makes three claims:

- "Good" is indefinable,
- there are objective moral truths, and
- the basic moral truths are self-evident to a mature mind.

I'll try to explain what these mean and why we should accept them.

Moore started with a simple question: What does the word "good" mean? This question is the key to understanding morality. If we answer it wrongly, we'll get everything wrong. So what does "good" mean? The answer, simply, is that "good" means "good." We can't define "good." "Good" is a simple idea, and we can't break it down into simpler ideas.

You may be thinking, "Surely all ideas are definable – and so 'good' must be definable." But, sorry, that's wrong. There *must* be indefinable ideas; we can't define every term without circularity. Suppose that we look up a word in the dictionary, and the word is defined using other words, and these are defined using still other words, and so on. Now there's only a limited number of words. So if we exclude circular definitions, then we'll eventually find words that we can't define further.

A nice example of an indefinable idea is the term "not." We can't define "not" using anything simpler. "Not" is a simple building block that we use to define other ideas. Saying that an idea is indefinable doesn't mean that it's difficult or obscure ("not" is neither of these), but just that it can't be broken down further.

I claim that "good," like "not," is a simple indefinable idea. Some philosophers disagree with this, and try to define "good." Some say that "good" means "socially approved." Others say that it means "liked," "pleasant," or even "desired by God." But these ideas are different from "good." "Good" simply means "good."

Moore had an argument to refute any proposed definition of "good." Let me show how it works. Some of my superficial friends are attracted to this definition:

> "Good" means "socially approved."

Every definition has two parts – the left part (the term defined) and the right part (the equivalent expression). A definition claims that the two parts are interchangeable in normal speech – that we can substitute one for the other without changing the meaning. We can test a definition by asking if one part necessarily applies whenever the other does. Here we'd ask, "Are socially approved things necessarily good?" The answer is a clear "no" – which refutes the definition. It's easy to imagine some bad things being socially approved. For our argument, it need only be *consistent* to imagine things that aren't good being socially approved. Since this clearly is consistent, the definition is wrong.

Moore's argument can refute any definition of "good." Suppose that someone defines "X is good" as "I desire X." We should ask, "Are things that I desire necessarily good?" The answer clearly is "no," which refutes the definition. We can refute other definitions of "good" in a similar way. The general strategy is this: if someone claims that "good" means "such and such" (where this represents some descriptive term), ask "Are things that are such and such necessarily good?" Since the answer is "no," the definition is refuted.

Naturalism is the view that "good" can be defined using ideas from sense experience (like "socially approved" or "desired"). Moore's argument refutes naturalism; but it also works against supernaturalism. All these views confuse evaluative with non-evaluative terms. Calling a thing "socially approved" (or whatever) puts it in a descriptive category; asking whether it's "good" asks about its value, which is different.

Since "good" is indefinable, we can't prove moral conclusions from non-moral premises alone. This result is called **Hume's law** (after the eighteenth-century philosopher David Hume). It says that we can't deduce an "ought" from an "is." In other words, we need a moral premise to deduce a moral conclusion. So this reasoning is incorrect (since it would work only if we could define "ought" using social approval):

> Society demands that you do such and such.
> ∴ You ought to do such and such.

This is bad reasoning, because it's consistent to affirm the premises and deny the conclusion. And the same thing goes if we substitute other descriptive premises.

Hume's law shows that we can't prove moral truths from descriptive facts alone. We can't give facts about society (or evolution, or God, or desires, or whatever) – and then from these alone logically deduce a moral conclusion. We could always consistently accept the facts and yet reject the moral conclusion. It follows that neither science nor religion can establish the basic principles of morality.

4.2 Objective truths

This is still Ima. I need another section to explain my claim that there are objective moral truths – moral truths that don't depend on human thinking or feeling.

"Hatred is wrong" is an example of an objective moral truth. The wrongness of hatred doesn't depend on what anyone may think or feel. Hatred is wrong in itself. It would still be wrong even if everyone approved of it. "Hatred is wrong" is a necessary truth – just like "x = x" or "2+2 = 4."

The belief in objective values is common sense. In our lives, we all assume that there's a correct answer to moral questions, that there's a truth to be discovered about right and wrong. But some, in their theories, deny objective values. They say, for example, that good and bad depend on what we like (subjectivism) or on what is socially approved (cultural relativism). But Moore's arguments refute their views.

I can't prove to you that values are objective any more than I can prove to you that there's a real world out there (and that we aren't just dreaming or hallucinating). Both beliefs are part of common sense, are clearly true, and need no proof. Let those who deny objective moral truths try to prove their case; I will refute their arguments.

And so I contend that the basic moral truths are necessary truths – things that are true of their very nature and that couldn't have been false. Let me add that this objective approach, while philosophically traditional, is politically radical. People who start revolutions are usually convinced of the *objective wrongness* of the current situation.

4.3   Self-evident truths

This is still Ima. I need another section to explain how we can know moral truths. My explanation is simple: we look within and follow the principles that seem most clearly self-evident to our minds. In a dispute, we defend our moral judgments by appealing to moral principles that are more basic. When we get to a rock-bottom principle, we can't defend it further. At this point, we see the principle or we don't.

Intuitionism is the commonsense approach. Relatively few people speak explicitly of "moral intuitions" or "self-evident moral truths." But many people appeal to moral principles that they take to be objective but not further provable or justifiable. Such people assume an intuitionist approach to morality, even though they might not call it that.

As a future lawyer, I admire the American Declaration of Independence, which lays down a firm foundation for government. This document appeals to self-evident truths as the foundation for morality:

> We hold these truths to be self-evident, that all men are created equal, that they are endowed by their Creator with certain unalienable Rights, that among these are Life, Liberty, and the pursuit of Happiness.

Note the objective language. The right to liberty is a self-evident truth. It isn't just something that we personally like, or that our culture approves of. Morality is based on objective truths that are present inside of us, in our own minds and reason. Any mature person should be able to grasp the basic moral truths.

A **self-evident truth** (or **first principle**) is a known truth that requires no further proof or justification. If you think about it, you'll see that morality has to be based on self-evident truths. Let's assume that (1) some moral truths are known, (2) we can only prove a moral truth by appealing to a more basic moral truth, and (3) our proofs can't continue forever. It follows that (4) the basic moral truths are known but not provable – they are self-evident truths.

I see only two ways to evade this reasoning. Premise (1) would be rejected by skeptics; they deny moral knowledge just as they deny our knowledge of the external world. But sensible people believe in common sense rather than in skeptics. Premise (2) would be denied by those who define "good" using descriptive ideas like "socially approved"; they say we can deduce moral truths from descriptive facts alone. But Moore's argument refutes such views and establishes Hume's law, which shows that we need a moral premise to deduce a moral conclusion.

Our opponents often misinterpret intuitionism. Some of them picture us as claiming that *all* moral truths are self-evident, that to resolve a moral issue you just sit down and have a moral intuition. But nothing could be further from the truth. We hold that only the basic moral principles are self-evident. To apply these basic principles to concrete problems requires further information. It's never just self-evident what we ought to do in a concrete situation.

What moral truths are self-evident? The great intuitionists Moore and Ross accepted two kinds of self-evident moral truth. First, there are truths about what is **intrinsically good** (what is good in itself, abstracting from further consequences). Here Moore and Ross agreed: it's self-evident that pleasure, knowledge, and virtue are intrinsically good – while pain, ignorance, and vice are intrinsically bad. A specific pleasure might have painful consequences, and so be bad in the final account; but still the pleasure aspect of it is good. "Pleasure is intrinsically better than pain" is as self-evident as anything could ever be.

Moore and Ross also accepted self-evident truths about duty; but here they disagreed. Moore thought it self-evident that we ought to do whatever maximizes good consequences for everyone. To determine our duty in a concrete case, we have to (1) determine our options, (2) determine the consequences of each option, and (3) evaluate which consequences are best. Steps (1) and (2) involve ordinary knowledge. Step (3) applies self-evident truths about intrinsic goodness – for example, that pleasure is intrinsically good. So we can't just sit down and have a self-evident intuition about what we ought to do. Instead, we must study options and consequences, and then appraise the consequences.

Ross rejected Moore's consequentialist approach. Ross claimed as self-evident a whole set of moral rules; other things being equal, we ought to keep our promises, not harm others, and so forth. I don't want to discuss this dispute now. [It will be dealt with later in the book.] I'll just note that intuitionists sometimes disagree about what moral principles are self-evident. The final appeal is to our intuition – to what seems true to us; but we must first carefully examine the alternatives. On the basis of our moral intuitions, I'd argue that Ross's view is better than Moore's.

Some of our opponents oppose intuitionism, because they think that self-evident truths would have to be present from birth and universally agreed upon – while moral principles are neither. But this shows a misunderstanding.

Let's think about how self-evident principles work in math. Consider this principle:

$$x+y = y+x$$

This is plausible initially, and remains plausible if we try concrete values for "x" and "y." For example, if we substitute "2" and "5" for "x" and "y," then we get "2+5 = 5+2," which simplifies to the true "7 = 7." So we find, after examination, that the formula fits our mathematical intuitions. So we regard it as a self-evident truth.

This principle also is plausible initially:

$$-(x \bullet y) = (-x \bullet -y)$$

But we get wrong results if we substitute "2" for "x" and "y." We get "-(2 • 2) = (-2 • -2)," which simplifies down to the false "-4 = +4." So we reject the formula, since it clashes with our mathematical intuitions.

These examples teach us two things. First, we can be mistaken in taking something to be a self-evident truth. We need to investigate whether a principle that sounds good has absurd implications.

Second, self-evident truths needn't be present from birth or universally agreed upon. Our formula "x+y = y+x" is neither of these. Babies and the uneducated won't grasp it, since they lack mathematical sophistication. Moral principles work the same way.

To arrive at self-evident principles, whether in math or in morality, requires reflection and intellectual maturity. The test of such principles isn't their initial plausibility, but whether a careful examination uncovers implications that clash with our intuitions.

And so I claim that we have self-evident principles in ethics just as we have them in math. To the mature mind, "Pleasure is intrinsically better than pain" is as self-evident as "x+y = y+x." Both are clear to almost any reflective, intelligent adult who has studied the matter. So there's no reason to trust our minds in one area but not the other.

Before closing, I should say something about moral education. We take a commonsense approach. Parents and other adults should know the basic truths about right and wrong. They should teach these truths to children by their own example, by verbal instruction, by praise and blame, and by reward and punishment. Moral education is difficult because children are swayed so easily by their feelings and by peer pressures; we have to struggle against these. Eventually, we hope, our children will grow up and become mature enough to recognize in their own hearts and minds the truth of the principles that we taught them.

Before going to Section 4.4, reflect on your initial reaction to intuitionism. What do you like or dislike about the view? Do you have any objections?

4.4 Objections

Ima has given us a clear formulation of an important approach to morality. I agree with much of what he says. Along with most philosophers today, I agree that "good" can't be defined using descriptive ideas. I also agree that there are objective moral truths – even though this is more disputed; we'll consider contrary views in the next two chapters. But the weakest part of Ima's view, in my opinion, is how he bases moral knowledge on moral intuitions and self-evident truths.

Ima says that we know the basic principles of math and of morality in the same way. Both are evident to the mature mind but need no proof. Is there any reason to trust our minds in one area but not the other? Unfortunately, there is. In math, the principles are *precise* and *largely agreed on* by the experts. In ethics, the principles are *vague* and *widely disputed*.

First, consider precision. The mathematical "x+y = y+x" uses precise, abstract terms and is exceptionless. By contrast, the moral "Pleasure is intrinsically good" uses vague ideas and has many exceptions. What exactly is pleasure? To see that the idea is vague, set the timer on your watch to go off every hour. When it goes off, ask yourself "Am I experiencing pleasure now, and, if so, how much?" Often you'll be perplexed on how to answer. Also, the principle needs qualifications. Is pleasure over the misfortune of another intrinsically good? Surely not. We can only say that pleasure is *normally* intrinsically good. So most moral principles are vague and have exceptions. In this they are very unlike mathematical principles.

Next consider agreement. Reflective, intelligent people who have studied math almost universally accept "x+y = y+x." By contrast, reflective, intelligent people who have studied ethics disagree widely about basic moral principles. In ethics, what seems self-evident to one person may seem absurd to another.

Intuitionists themselves disagree about what moral principles are self-evident. (1) Some accept one big rule about duty. Of these, some prefer a rule like Moore's, that we ought to do whatever maximizes good consequences for everyone. Others take egoism to be self-evident, that we ought to do whatever maximizes good consequences for ourselves. (2) Some take a set of rules about duty to be self-evident. Some hold exceptionless rules – for example, that killing a human fetus is always wrong, or that killing a human fetus is always permissible. Ross takes as self-evident only weaker principles that hold other things being equal; he rejects exceptionless principles. There are many disputes about these principles. (3) Some take as self-evident only concrete judgments of duty, that in this concrete situation I ought to do such and such.

Moral intuitions come largely from social conditioning. The norms that we were taught as children become our "moral intuitions" later on. So if we're brought up in a racist society, then we'll likely have racist intuitions. Since moral intuitions vary so much between cultures, it's hard to imagine that they're a reliable guide to an objective moral truth. The situation is quite different in math, since reflective, intelligent people of all cultures who have studied math almost universally accept principles like "x+y = y+x" and "x = x."

Intuitionism can lead to an early stalemate on moral issues. Consider people who were brought up in a Nazi society. It may seem "self-evident" to them that Jews ought to be treated poorly – while it seems "self-evident" to us that all people ought to be treated with respect. Intuitionism can't carry the argument any further. How is this any better than subjectivism? Despite the appearance of rationality, intuitionism isn't much different in practice from subjectivism.

Consider Ima's approach to moral education. He wants us to teach our children whatever principles seem self-evident to us. We can teach such principles by parental example, verbal instruction, and reward and punishment. This is fine, but incomplete, since the same methods can teach bigotry. Our parental example can teach that Jews are to be hated;

and we can praise our children when they follow our example and punish them when they act kindly toward Jews. If such moral training succeeds, our children will end up internalizing Nazi values. It will seem "self-evident" to them that Jews ought to be hated.

We need some rational way to criticize our inherited moral intuitions. Intuitionism doesn't tell us how to do this – or how to distinguish "genuine" from "apparent" moral intuitions.

4.5   Reconstruction

Intuitionism tells us to pick out our moral principles by following our basic moral intuitions. We saw problems with this. But suppose that we still believe in irreducible, objective moral truths. Is there any other way that we could know such truths – a way that doesn't just appeal to moral intuitions? Could perhaps some other approach help us to criticize our inherited moral intuitions and to arrive at objective moral knowledge?

I can suggest two possibilities. Maybe we could search more deeply for moral principles that are precise and almost universally accepted among intelligent people who have studied ethics. Or maybe we could get help from the method used in the ideal observer view (see Chapter 2). We'll explore both possibilities later, in Chapters 7 to 9.

Or perhaps we should throw out the idea of objective moral truths – and instead try to build ethics on a different basis. The next two chapters suggest ways to do this.

4.6   Chapter summary

Intuitionism makes three claims: (1) "Good" is indefinable, (2) there are objective moral truths, and (3) the basic moral truths are self-evident to a mature mind. Let me explain these claims.

(1) "Good" is a simple, indefinable notion. Suppose that someone defines "good" as "socially approved." We should ask, "Are socially approved things necessarily good?" The answer clearly is "no," which refutes the definition. We can refute other definitions of "good" in a similar way. Since "good" is indefinable, we can't prove moral conclusions from non-moral premises alone.

(2) There are objective moral truths – moral truths that don't depend on human thinking or feeling. "Hatred is wrong" is an example. Hatred is wrong in itself. It would still be wrong even if everyone approved of it. It's an objective truth that hatred is wrong.

(3) The basic moral principles are self-evident truths – known truths that require no further proof or justification. To apply these to concrete actions requires further information; it's never self-evident what we ought to do in a concrete situation. To arrive at the self-evident principles of morality requires reflection and intellectual maturity. The test of such principles isn't their initial plausibility, but whether a careful examination uncovers implications that clash with our intuitions.

Intuitionism, despite its initial plausibility, has some problems. In math, principles claimed to be self-evident are precise and largely agreed on by the experts. In ethics, principles claimed to be self-evident are vague and widely disputed. Intuitionists themselves disagree widely about what is self-evident.

Moral intuitions come largely from social conditioning, and vary greatly between cultures. So it's hard to imagine that such intuitions are a reliable guide to objective moral truths. And appealing to intuitions can lead to an early stalemate on moral issues – as when we argue with someone who has racist intuitions.

4.7   Study questions

Write out the answers in your ethics folder. If you don't know an answer, go back to the section that deals with it.

1. How does intuitionism define "good"? What method does it follow for arriving at moral principles?
2. Why must there be indefinable terms? What example did Ima give of an indefinable term? (4.1)
3. Consider the subjectivist definition, that "X is good" means "I like X." How would Moore argue against it?
4. Consider the supernaturalist definition, that "X is good" means "The creator of the world desires X." How would Moore argue against it?
5. What is Hume's law? Why would it show that neither science nor religion can establish basic moral principles?
6. Explain Ima's claim that there are objective moral truths. Why does he believe in such truths? (4.2)
7. What is a self-evident truth? How did Ima argue that morality must be based on self-evident truths? (4.3)
8. Why can't we decide what we ought to do in a concrete situation by just sitting down and having a moral intuition?

9. Give an example of a principle about intrinsic goodness that Moore and Ross both took to be self-evident.
10. What principles of duty did Moore take to be self-evident? What principles of duty did Ross take to be self-evident?
11. Do self-evident principles have to be present from birth and universally agreed upon? Talk about "x+y = y+x."
12. Should we accept as self-evident any principle that seems initially plausible to us? Talk about "-(x • y) = (-x • -y)."
13. What approach did Ima take to moral education?
14. Write about a page sketching your initial reaction to intuitionism. Does it seem plausible to you? What do you like and dislike about it? Can you think of any way to show that it's false?
15. In what two ways are basic principles of math claimed to be unlike basic principles of morality? (4.4)
16. Do intuitionists agree about what moral principles are self-evident? Give some examples of such disagreements.
17. Explain how moral intuitions are claimed to come from social conditioning – and how appealing to moral intuitions can lead to a stalemate in arguing with a racist.
18. What objection is made to Ima's approach to moral education?
19. What two ways are suggested for reconstructing intuitionism? (4.5)

4.8 For further study

To solidify your understanding, do the computer exercises for "Ethics 04 – Intuitionism." The Computer Exercises appendix at the end of this book has further information on this and on Internet resources.

The classic defenses of intuitionism are Moore's *Principia Ethica* (especially the preface and first chapter) and Ross's *The Right and the Good*. Some philosophers of a broadly intuitionist perspective think that we grasp moral truths by a kind of perception that resembles sense experience; Werner's "Ethical realism" is an example. An exact statement of Hume's law requires various qualifications; see page 67 of Gensler's *Formal Ethics*. The Bibliography at the end of the book has information on how to find these works.

CHAPTER 5
Emotivism

CHAPTER 5
Emotivism

Emotivism:

"X is good" is an emotional exclamation (not a truth claim), and means "Hurrah for X!"

Pick out your moral principles by following your feelings.

Emotivism says that moral judgments express positive or negative feelings. "X is good" is equivalent to the exclamation "Hurrah for X!" – and hence can't be true or false. So there can't be moral truths or moral knowledge.

We'll begin by listening to the fictional Ima Emotivist explain her belief in emotivism. Then we'll take objections.

5.1 Ima Emotivist

My name is Ima Emotivist. I've embraced emotivism as I've learned that moral judgments express only feelings, and not true or false judgments.

Let me tell you how I came to emotivism. I'm a double-major in philosophy and chemistry, with a special interest in philosophy of science. The British A.J. Ayer is my favorite philosopher. Like Ayer, I respect the scientific method, which I see as the only way to gain knowledge about the world. Scientific method has you propose a view and then do experiments to see if your view is correct. A view must be testable by sense experience – or else it makes no sense. This is the idea behind Ayer's philosophy, which he called **logical positivism**.

I'm oversimplifying here. To get more precise, I must bring in some technical terms; I hope that I don't bore you. Logical positivism holds that only two types of statement make genuine **truth claims** (claims that are true or false). First, there are **empirical statements**; these can in principle be shown by our sense experience to be true or at least highly probable. Second, there are **analytic statements**; these are true because of the meaning of words. Here are examples:

Empirical (testable by sense experience): "It's snowing outside."	**Analytic** (true by definition): "All bachelors are single."

The empirical statement can be tested by sense experience; you go outside and look for snow. The analytic statement is true by definition, since we use "bachelor" to mean "single man"; so we don't need to study bachelors to see that the statement is true. In general, science is empirical while mathematics is analytic. I hope that you get the idea.

Logical positivism claims that any genuine truth claim is either empirical (testable by sense experience) or analytic (true by definition). If your statement isn't one of these two sorts, then it's meaningless. Let me give an example. Suppose that you say "True reality is spiritual" – but your claim isn't empirical (testable by sense experience) or analytic (true by definition). Then you aren't saying anything that could be true or false. You may perhaps be expressing feelings. But you aren't making a truth claim if what you say isn't empirical or analytic.

How would logical positivism apply to ethics? Is ethics empirical? Can "X is good," like statements of chemistry, be tested by sense experience? It seems not.

We should perhaps slow down here. **Naturalism** claims that "good" can be defined using ideas from sense experience. For example, cultural relativism defines "good" as "socially approved." If this definition worked, then "X is good" would be a genuine empirical statement; we could test its truth by testing whether X was socially approved. So this definition would make ethics a branch of sociology. Unfortunately, however, such definitions don't work. "Good" in our language doesn't mean "socially approved," since it's consistent to say that some socially approved things aren't good. This point should be familiar if you know about Moore's famous refutation of naturalism.

So moral judgments aren't empirical; moral principles can't be proved or disproved by sense experience. Are they analytic (true by definition)? It seems not. So moral judgments are neither empirical nor analytic. It follows that they express, not genuine truth claims, but at most our feelings about things.

This is Ayer's reasoning, and I think that it's solid. If we accept a scientific attitude toward the world, then we're inescapably led to the emotivist approach to ethics.

However, the scientific attitude isn't the only road to emotivism. My boyfriend is an English major, and cares nothing about science. But he loved emotivism when I explained it to him. He said that making "good" emotional brought it closer to the realm of poetry (his true love) and away from "cold, impersonal science." He liked emotivism right away and didn't even want to hear my reasoning in defense of it.

5.2   "Good" is emotional

This is still Ima. I need another section to explain more clearly what emotivism holds.

Emotivism sees a moral judgment as an expression of feeling, not a statement that's literally true or false. Moral judgments are exclamations: "X is good" means "Hurrah for X!" – and "X is bad" means "Boo on X!" An exclamation doesn't state any fact, and isn't true or false. Since moral judgments are exclamations, there can't be moral truths or moral knowledge.

Don't take "hurrah" and "boo" literally. English has many words to express positive or negative feelings. Instead of "boo," we could say "hiss," "yeech," or "tsk tsk"; or we might shake our finger in disapproval. These express different shades of feeling and fit different contexts. There might not be any English exclamation exactly equivalent to "bad" (although we could invent one if we wished). The main point is that "bad" expresses negative feelings, as does "boo," and functions like an exclamation.

Don't confuse our view with subjectivism. We hold that moral judgments express feelings but don't assert truths about feelings. These examples may make my distinction clearer:

Just express feelings (emotivism):	*Truths about feelings (subjectivism):*
"Brrr!"	"I feel cold."
"Ha, ha!"	"I find that funny."
"Wow!"	"I'm impressed."
"Hurrah for X!"	"I like X."

Suppose that you say "Brrr!" as you shiver in the cold. Your "Brrr!" isn't literally true or false; it would be out of place to respond to it by saying "That's true." Now suppose that you say "I feel cold." Here you're saying something true – since you *do* feel cold. A moral judgment is like "Brrr!" (which just expresses your feelings), and not like "I feel cold" (which is a truth claim about your feelings).

This distinction lets us avoid some problems that subjectivism has. Suppose that Hitler, who likes the killing of Jews, says "The killing of Jews is good." On subjectivism, Hitler's statement is *true* (since it just means that he likes the killing of Jews). This is bizarre. We think Hitler's statement is an exclamation ("Hurrah for the killing of Jews!"), and thus not true or false. We can't say that Hitler's moral judgment is false; but at least we don't have to say that it's true.

While moral judgments express our personal feelings, they also have social functions. We often use moral judgments to influence people's emotions and to stimulate action. For example, I say to my baby sister, "It's *good* to pick up our toys." I'm trying to get her to have positive feelings about picking up her toys – and to act accordingly.

Sometimes we use moral judgments to influence *ourselves*. When the alarm went off this morning, I had to get up for chemistry lab; but I felt like staying in bed. So I said to myself, "It's *good* to get up now!" This is like saying, "Hurrah for getting up now!" Part of me is a cheerleader, trying to influence the other part. Deep inside of me, different emotions fight for supremacy. To take another example, I sometimes feel like being nasty to someone, but part of me says "That's bad – boo!"

Before closing this section, let me give you another strong argument for my approach. Emotivism is better than the other views because it's simpler and explains more of the facts. In philosophy, as in science, a view is better if it's simpler and explains more.

First, emotivism explains morality more simply. Evaluative judgments express positive or negative feelings. What could be simpler? We don't bring in things that are difficult to defend. Supernaturalists have to defend belief in God – with all the difficulties that that has. And intuitionists have to defend objective, irreducible moral facts. Suppose that you're a materialist; you hold that all facts about the universe are ultimately expressible in the language of physics and chemistry. How do objective, irreducible moral facts fit into such a universe? Are moral facts composed of chemicals, or what sort of weird thing are they? And how could we ever know such mysterious facts? Emotivism avoids these problems and thus explains morality more simply.

Second, emotivism explains more of the facts about morality. The reason we can't define "good" in purely descriptive terms is that "good" is emotional. The reason we can't resolve basic moral differences intellectually is that these differences are emotional (and so not purely intellectual). The reason we humans differ so much in our moral beliefs is that we have different feelings about things. Once we take the emotivist view, morality becomes more understandable.

Finally, emotivism accurately explains what we mean by "good" and "bad." Yesterday I was at a restaurant with my boyfriend. Just for fun, we switched from "good" to "hurrah," and from "bad" to "boo." It felt funny at first, but it made sense. We could express everything that we wanted to say. And we didn't feel that we changed what we were talking about (as we would if we switched from "good" to "socially approved" or "desired by God"). So emotivism is accurate linguistically. If you doubt this, try the same experiment yourself; but don't be surprised if the waiter gives you a funny look.

5.3   Moral reasoning

This is still Ima. I need a third section to explain to you how emotivism handles moral reasoning.

We can reason about moral issues if we assume a system of norms. We can then appeal to empirical facts to show that, given these norms and these empirical facts, such and such a moral conclusion follows. Suppose that we all feel that lying is wrong; we can then appeal to empirical facts (that the president lied) to establish a moral conclusion (that the president acted wrongly). This kind of reasoning can be useful within a group that shares common norms.

We can't reason about *basic* moral principles. We can use emotional means at this point – but not reason. Imagine that you're arguing with a Nazi. You'll likely disagree on some basic moral principle. Maybe you hold that all races are to be treated with respect, while he thinks that his race is to be treated better. We see this as a difference in feelings, while intuitionists see it as a difference in moral intuitions. But neither view can progress further by reasoning. So intuitionism has no practical advantage over emotivism. Instead, emotivism has the advantage, since it shows that we can go further by appealing, not to reason, but to emotion. To convince the Nazi, we have to make him *feel* differently about other races. We have to change his hatred and hostility into feelings of friendship or toleration.

With moral education too, we take the same approach as intuitionists, except that we talk about feelings instead of truths. As parents, we should first get clear on our feelings about how to live; then we can teach these to our children by personal example, by verbal instruction, by praise and blame, and by reward and punishment. If our teaching succeeds, our children will share our feelings about how to live. But nothing prevents them from changing their feelings later on.

People sometimes claim that emotivism would destroy morality and the moral life. But this is mistaken. We emotivists for the most part live out our values in the same way as do intuitionists. The main difference is that we don't think that there's anything objective behind our values. We see morality as about feelings, not about truths. But we can still feel strongly about our values.

> Before going to Section 5.4, reflect on your initial reaction to emotivism. What do you like or dislike about the view? Do you have any objections?

5.4 Positivism problems

Ima Emotivist has given a clear formulation of an important approach to morality. Her view presents a challenge for those of us who want to believe in moral truths and moral knowledge, and who hope for a stronger role for reason in ethics.

Ima's belief in logical positivism led her to emotivism. We can formulate her argument as follows:

> Any genuine truth claim is either empirical (testable by sense experience) or analytic (true by definition).
> Moral statements aren't either empirical or analytic.
> ∴ Moral statements aren't genuine truth claims.

The problem here is that the first premise, the central claim of logical positivism, is self-refuting. Let's assume that the first premise is true. Is the premise empirical (testable by sense experience)? It seems not. Is it analytic (true by definition)? Again, it seems not. So, on its own terms, it isn't a genuine truth claim – and thus can't be true. So the premise is self-refuting; if we assume that it's true, we can show that it isn't true.

To see the objection more clearly, consider Ima's rough formulation of logical positivism:

> A view must be testable by sense experience
> – or else it makes no sense.

This claim itself can't be tested by sense experience. But then, on its own terms, it makes no sense. So the claim is self-refuting.

Philosophers who worship science often contradict themselves. They make claims, which can't be based on science, about science being the only path to the truth. Such philosophers violate our first duty as rational beings, which is, not the impossible demand that we prove all our claims, but the humble demand that our claims be consistent with each other.

Ayer and the other logical positivists were logical people. They gave up their view when they saw it was self-refuting. Their view had other problems too; for example, it proved impossible to give a clear definition of "empirical." Few philosophers today accept logical positivism.

5.5 Other objections

Even though logical positivism died many years ago, emotivism still prospers. Ima explains emotivism's main attraction:

> Emotivism is better than the other views because it's simpler and explains more of the facts. In philosophy, as in science, a view is better if it's simpler and explains more.

I grant that emotivism explains morality in a simple way. But the truth isn't always simple, and emotivism seems to water down what morality is. In denying moral knowledge and moral truth, it goes against common sense. But we've done poorly so far in defending our knowledge of basic moral truths. Are such truths self-evident? The wide variation in moral intuitions casts doubt on this. Or are they provable from descriptive facts? Moore seems to have destroyed this approach. As long as we can't find a better way to defend our knowledge of moral truths, views that deny such knowledge will remain plausible.

In view of this, we might look for internal problems with emotivism. I find two such problems. Contrary to what emotivism says, moral judgments aren't always emotional and don't always translate plausibly into exclamations.

First, moral judgments aren't always emotional. We all have some moral beliefs that are emotional for us (maybe about racism) and others that are unemotional (maybe about the wrongness of some tax exemptions). Since moral judgments may be very unemotional, it's implausible to equate them all with exclamations – like "Boo!" and "Hurrah!" – whose main purpose is to express emotion.

Since Ima Emotivist likes science so much, she might do an experiment to see if moral judgments are always emotional. She could interview people, hook up some gismo to measure their emotions, and then test whether moral judgments are always emotional (as emotivism holds) or go from highly emotional to highly unemotional (as I hold). I have no doubt about how the experiment would turn out.

A second problem is that "good" and "bad" don't always translate plausibly into exclamations. Consider these examples:

1.   Do what is good.
2.   Hurrah for good people!
3.   Either it's good to go or it's bad to go.
4.   This is neutral (neither good nor bad).

Here's what we get if we replace "good" and "bad" with exclamations:

1a.   Do what is hurrah!
2a.   Hurrah for hurrah! people!
3a.   Either hurrah for going! or boo on going!
4a.   Neither hurrah for this! nor boo on this!

If we use exclamations in the normal way, none of these translations make sense. So some sentences using "good" and "bad" seem to have no plausible "hurrah" and "boo" equivalents.

Subjectivists can plausibly translate my four sentences. For example, they'd translate sentence 1 into "Do what I like" or "Do what I'd say 'Hurrah!' to." But this makes "X is good" into a truth claim about feelings – and emotivists reject this. Emotivists claim that "good" translates into an exclamation.

There's yet another problem. In defending emotivism, Ima appeals to this principle, which is an important part of scientific method:

•   A view is *better* if it's simpler and explains more.

Now "better" is the comparative of "good." So if "good" translates into an exclamation, then Ima's principle means something like this:

•   Hurrah for a view that's simpler and explains more!

So Ima's principle would be a mere expression of feeling – and thus not true or false. And the same would go for other norms that are part of scientific method:

- We *ought* normally to believe our sense experience.
- In our scientific theories, we *ought* to be consistent.

These too, if they're just exclamations, wouldn't be true or false; so they'd be no more correct than these two norms:

- A view is *better* if it accords with my horoscope.
- We *ought* to decide between scientific views by flipping a coin.

So emotivism, besides destroying the objectivity of ethics, would also seem to destroy the objectivity of scientific method.

5.6   Moderate emotivism

What disturbs me most about emotivism is its claim that we can't reason about basic moral principles.

Suppose that we disagree with a Nazi on a basic moral principle. Emotivism says that we can't progress further by reasoning; but we can try to change the Nazi's feelings. However, the Nazi also can try to change *our* feelings; historically, Nazis were very good at manipulating feelings. So the emotivist model of moral thinking would seem to lead to propaganda wars, in which each side, unable to resort to reason, simply tries to manipulate the feelings of the other side. I find this disturbing.

Ima says that intuitionism can't reason about basic moral principles either. We can't argue about *basic intuitions* any more than we can about *basic feelings*. She concludes that emotivism and intuitionism are in the same boat. If so, I'd like to be in a different boat from both of them; I want some method whereby both sides could sit down and reason together, instead of just trying to manipulate each other's emotions.

Some emotivists try to bring more rationality into ethics. They move to **moderate emotivism**. This view still sees moral judgments as emotional exclamations, and not truth claims. But it insists that feelings can be rationally appraised to some degree: *rational feelings* are ones that are informed and impartial. On these grounds, we could argue that the Nazi's principles are irrational. This approach works much like the ideal observer view (see Chapter 2). We'd pick out our moral principles by following our feelings – but we'd first develop rational feelings (ones that are informed and impartial).

Moderate emotivism gives a larger role to rationality in ethics. Hare's prescriptivism, which we'll consider in the next chapter, goes further in the same direction.

5.7 Chapter summary

Emotivism says that moral judgments express positive or negative feelings. "X is good" means "Hurrah for X!" – and "X is bad" means "Boo on X!"

Since moral judgments are exclamations, they can't be true or false. So there can't be moral truths or moral knowledge. We can reason about moral issues if we assume a system of norms; but we can't reason about basic moral principles.

Some emotivists base their view on logical positivism, which holds roughly that any genuine truth claim must be able to be tested by sense experience. Since moral judgments can't be tested by sense experience, they aren't genuine truth claims. So moral judgments only express feelings. Thus logical positivism leads to emotivism.

One problem with this argument is that logical positivism is self-refuting. It claims (roughly) "Any genuine truth claim must be able to be tested by sense experience." But this claim itself can't be tested by sense experience. So, by its own standard, logical positivism can't be a genuine truth claim.

Others argue that emotivism is better than the other approaches because it's simpler and explains more of the facts. They appeal to this principle, which is an important part of scientific method: "A view is better if it's simpler and explains more."

However, it isn't clear that emotivism explains morality adequately; by denying moral knowledge and moral truth, it seems to water down what morality is. Another problem is that moral judgments, instead of being essentially emotional, go from "very emotional" to "not very emotional." And moral judgments don't always translate plausibly into exclamations.

Emotivism also would seem to destroy the objectivity of scientific method – since it would translate "A scientific view is better if it's simpler and explains more" into the exclamation "Hurrah for scientific views that are simpler and explain more!"

Emotivism claims that, in disputes about basic moral principles, we can't appeal to reason but only to emotion. This would seem to lead to propaganda wars in which each side, unable to resort to reason, simply tries to manipulate the feelings of the other side.

Moderate emotivism tries to add a stronger rationality component. While admitting that ethics is based on feelings, it insists that our feelings can be more or less rational to the extent that we're informed and impartial.

5.8   Study questions

Write out the answers in your ethics folder. If you don't know an answer, go back to the section that deals with it.

1. How does emotivism define "good"? What method does it follow for arriving at moral beliefs?
2. Define these terms: "truth claim," "empirical statement," and "analytic statement." (5.1)
3. Explain what logical positivism is and how it led Ima to accept emotivism.
4. Why did Ima reject definitions of "good" that use empirical language (such as "socially approved")?
5. Why did Ima's boyfriend accept emotivism?
6. Explain how emotivism and subjectivism differ. (5.2)
7. Suppose that Hitler, who likes the killing of Jews, says "The killing of Jews is good." Would subjectivism say that Hitler's statement is true? Would emotivism say that it is true?
8. What social functions do moral judgments have?
9. Suppose that you don't feel like doing X. On emotivism, why might it still make sense for you to say to yourself, "It's good for me to do X"?
10. Why did Ima think that emotivism gives a simple explanation of morality?
11. According to emotivism, why can't we define "good" in descriptive terms?
12. What evidence did Ima give that emotivism is accurate linguistically?
13. In what ways can we reason on moral issues? How does the Nazi example show the limits of moral reasoning? (5.3)
14. How did Ima apply emotivism to moral education? Did she think that emotivism would destroy morality?
15. Write about a page sketching your initial reaction to emotivism. Does it seem plausible to you? What do you like and dislike about it? Can you think of any way to show that it's false?
16. What objection is given to logical positivism? (5.4)
17. Explain the objection that moral judgments aren't always emotional. (5.5)
18. Give some examples of sentences with "good" or "bad" that don't seem to translate into exclamations.
19. Explain the objection that emotivism would destroy the rationality of science.

20. How might the emotivist model of moral thinking lead to propaganda wars? (5.6)
21. What is moderate emotivism?

5.9 For further study

To solidify your understanding, do the computer exercises for "Ethics 05 – Emotivism." The Computer Exercises appendix at the end of this book has further information on this and on Internet resources.

Classic defenses of emotivism include Chapter 6 of Ayer's *Language, Truth and Logic* and Stevenson's longer *Facts and Values*. Recent defenses of emotivism include Blackburn's *Essays in Quasi-Realism* and Gibbard's *Wise Choices, Apt Feelings*. Also of interest is the related view in the first chapter of Mackie's *Ethics: Inventing Right and Wrong*. Frankena defends moderate emotivism in the last chapter of his *Ethics*.

Ayer's book mentioned above gives a classic defense of logical positivism. Also helpful are Passmore's brief "Logical positivism" and Ashby's brief "Verifiability principle." The Bibliography at the end of the book has information on how to find these works.

CHAPTER 6
Prescriptivism

CHAPTER 6
Prescriptivism

> **Prescriptivism:**
>
> "You ought to do this" is a universalizable pre-
> scription (not a truth claim); it means "Do this
> and let everyone do the same in similar cases."
>
> Pick out your moral principles by first trying to
> be informed and imaginative, and then seeing
> what you can consistently hold.

Prescriptivism sees ought judgments as a type of **prescription** (or imperative). "You *ought* to do A," like "Do A," doesn't state a fact and isn't true or false. Instead, it expresses our will, or our desires. But unlike simple imperatives, ought judgments are **universalizable**. This means that they logically commit us to making similar evaluations about similar cases. This leads to a useful form of golden rule reasoning.

We'll begin by listening to the fictional Ima Prescriptivist explain his belief in prescriptivism. Then we'll consider objections.

6.1 Ima Prescriptivist

My name is Ima Prescriptivist. I've embraced prescriptivism as I've come to see that moral judgments express our impartial desires about how people are to live.

I'm taking a moral philosophy course right now. Until last month, I hadn't found the views very attractive. Then we started R.M. Hare's prescriptivism. Hare's view makes more sense to me than all the others put together. I'll try to explain his view; but you'll have to bear with me, because it's complicated. You won't see its attractiveness until we get far into it.

Let me start at the beginning. An ought judgment is a type of pre-scription, or imperative. Compare these two examples:

Indicative:	*Imperative:*
The door is open.	Close the door.

The indicative tries to state a fact about the world, and is true or false. To accept the indicative is to have a belief. But the imperative doesn't state a fact, and isn't true or false. Instead, it tells what to do – it expresses our will, or our desire, that the person close the door. Moral judgments are like the imperative. They don't state facts, and aren't true or false. Instead, they express our will, or desires, about how people are to live. To accept a moral judgment isn't to have a belief about some external fact. Instead, it is to commit yourself to a way of life.

You're probably thinking, "Oh no, Ima rejects moral truths; so his view is going to be just like emotivism." But don't judge so quickly. My view makes ethics rational, and so is very *unlike* emotivism. It doesn't matter that moral judgments aren't literally true or false. What matters is that we can refute Nazi racists and teach our children how to think rationally about moral issues.

Imperatives can be highly rational and needn't be very emotional. Many impressive achievements of human reason are systems of impera-tives. Consider a cookbook with complicated recipes, our country's laws, the rules for chess, and the directions for using a complex computer program. A computer program itself consists of instructions that tell the computer what to do under various conditions. Imperatives can have a sophisticated logical structure and needn't be very emotional. By con-trast, exclamations are primitive grunts.

Moral judgments in our ordinary speech are closer to imperatives than to exclamations. In discussing ethics, we often shift between imperatives ("Don't kill") and ought judgments ("You ought not to kill"); the two seem similar. It would be strange to use exclamations ("Boo on killing!").

6.2 Freedom and reason

This is still Ima. Let me explain why I like prescriptivism.

To satisfy me, an ethical theory has to do two things. First, it has to allow me the *freedom* to form my own moral beliefs. Sure, I need factual information and advice from others. But these alone won't give me the answer. To think otherwise would compromise my freedom as a moral agent. In the end, I have to answer my own moral questions.

The worst approach to ethics is cultural relativism. This view gives you no freedom to think for yourself on moral issues. You have to go along with the crowd – with whatever the majority approves of. I can't accept this. I'm a free person, and I can think for myself about ethics.

In addition, a satisfying view has to show us how to be *rational* in forming our moral beliefs. Morality is important. It shouldn't be an arbitrary thing, like picking a postage stamp. Answering moral questions should engage our rational powers to their limits.

Subjectivism is an example of an irrational approach. Here you can say, "I like it – so it must be good." How idiotic! Don't we have minds? Can't we reason about morality?

But *how* can we reason about morality? None of the earlier views has been very helpful on this. Do we just go with our basic moral intuitions? What if our society has taught us racist intuitions? The ideal observer view gives the beginning of a rational approach, but it's too vague.

So a satisfying view should show us how to form our moral beliefs in a *free* and *rational* way. This reminds me of my younger brother, Brian. His girlfriend got him involved in a Nazi group that preaches racial hatred. So he talked with me about how we ought to treat other races. Brian asked, "Ima, don't just force your principles on me, but instead teach me how to think out my own moral views." He was confused on how to think out moral questions. He said that the alternative to *thinking* was to just go along with the side that most sways your emotions. Later I'll say how I answered his question.

So how can we be both free and rational in forming our moral beliefs? Hare struggled with this question and came up with a remarkably innovative answer. He sees moral language as the key. What do we mean by "ought"? Once we understand this term, we can discover the logical rules for its use. Then we can understand how to reason for ourselves about moral issues.

Hare sees ought judgments as universalizable prescriptions. "You ought to do this" is equivalent to "Do this and let everyone do the same in similar cases." Our moral beliefs express our desire that a kind of act be done in the present case and in all similar cases. Moral beliefs can be *free* because they express our own desires and aren't provable from facts. They can be *rational* because the logic of "ought" leads to a method of moral reasoning that engages our rational powers to their limits.

6.3 Moral reasoning

This is still Ima. I need to give the logical rules for "ought" – and then show how moral thinking can be rational.

There are two basic logical rules for "ought":

U. To be logically consistent, we must make similar evaluations about similar cases.

P. To be logically consistent, we must keep our moral beliefs in harmony with how we live and want others to live.

These rules are based on the meaning of "ought" – which is a word for expressing universalizable prescriptions. Rule U holds because ought judgments are universalizable: it's part of their meaning that they apply to similar cases. Rule P holds because ought judgments are prescriptions (imperatives), and thus express our will, or our desires, about how we and others are to live.

Rules U and P are consistency rules. They aren't imperatives or moral judgments. They don't say "We *ought* to do such and such ..." Instead, they tell us what we must do if we're to be logically consistent in our moral beliefs. These rules, despite their abstractness, are very useful. They lead to a golden rule (GR) consistency condition, which is the most important element in rational moral thinking.

Suppose that Detra has a nice bicycle – and I say to myself:

(a) I believe that I *ought* to steal Detra's bicycle.

By rule U, this logically commits me to making the same ought judgment about an imagined reversed situation:

(b) I believe that, if the situation were exactly reversed, then Detra *ought* to steal my bicycle.

By rule P, this in turn logically commits me to willing something about the imagined reversed situation:

(c) I desire that, if the situation were exactly reversed, then Detra would steal my bicycle.

So believing that I ought to steal Detra's bicycle logically commits me to desiring that my bicycle be stolen if I were in her place. If I don't desire this, then I'm inconsistent in holding my original ought judgment.

Here's a general formulation of this idea – which is somewhat like the traditional golden rule ("Treat others as you want to be treated"):

> The **GR consistency condition** claims that this combination is logically inconsistent:
>
> - I believe that I *ought* to do something to another.
> - I don't desire that this be done to me in the same situation.

This consistency condition holds because ought judgments are universalizable prescriptions. To accept an ought judgment in a consistent way is to desire that a kind of act be done in all similar cases, including ones where we imagine ourselves in the place of the other person.

To apply the GR consistency condition, we'd imagine ourselves in the exact place of the other person on the receiving end of the action. If we think we ought to do something to another, but don't desire that this be done to us in the same situation, then we violate GR consistency. Suppose that we think we ought to enslave others because of their skin color, but we don't desire that we be enslaved if we were in the same situation (including the same skin color). Then we're inconsistent – and we're breaking the logical rules built into the term "ought."

To apply our GR consistency condition most adequately, we need knowledge and imagination. We need to *know* what effect our actions have on the lives of others. And we need to *imagine* ourselves, vividly and accurately, in the other person's place on the receiving end of the action. GR consistency, when combined with knowledge and imagination, is an important tool for refuting Nazi racists and for teaching our children to think rationally about moral issues.

To think rationally about ethics, we need to be informed, imaginative, and consistent. Moral reasoning doesn't deduce moral conclusions from facts. Instead, it tests our consistency. The most important kind of moral consistency is GR consistency. If we think we ought to do something to another, but don't desire that this be done to us in an imagined identical situation, then we're inconsistent.

6.4 Against Nazis

This is still Ima. I need another section to tell you how I answered my younger brother's question.

Recall that my brother Brian got involved with a Nazi group that preached racial hatred. He was perplexed about how we ought to treat other races. He asked, "Ima, don't just force your principles on me, but instead teach me how to think out my own moral views." He was confused on how to *reason* about moral questions.

How did I answer? First I praised Brian for wanting to *reason* instead of just following his emotions. Emotions are great – but not Nazi emotions divorced from reason. Many Nazis don't want to be rational, and prefer violence or emotional rhetoric.

Then I told Brian that he had to make up his own mind on moral issues. Moral principles can't be proved or disproved by appealing to facts. The principles he accepted would be his own free choice, and would express how he wanted people to live.

Brian broke in, "Are you saying that we can't reason about basic moral principles?" I replied that I was *not* saying this. I told him that many philosophers had claimed that we can't reason about basic moral principles, but that Hare had shown them wrong. We can reason by appealing to consistency. Even though we're free to form our own moral beliefs, our beliefs can be more or less rational. To think rationally about ethics is to think in a way that is informed, imaginative, and consistent.

To be informed is to understand the facts correctly. So we talked about the facts. We talked about the differences between races, and whether these are genetic or cultural. We talked about how Nazism develops and spreads. We talked about alternatives to Nazi views, and how other societies deal with racial diversity. And we talked about the probable consequences of the Nazi strategy, and alternative strategies, on people's lives – including the lives of the Jews who would suffer under Nazi policies.

I told Brian that it wasn't enough just to know the facts; we also need to appreciate the human significance of the facts on people's lives. We need what Hare calls "imagination." So I told Brian to imagine himself and his family in the place of the victims, those who would suffer from Nazi policies.

I told Brian that we also need to be consistent, and I explained GR consistency. Brian saw right away that this would exclude Nazi policies. He said, "Surely I don't desire that I and my family be treated so badly if we were in the place of the Jews. So I can't consistently hold that I ought to treat them this way." He concluded that Nazi moral beliefs were irrational – since Nazis wouldn't hold these beliefs consistently if they knew the facts of the case and exercised their imagination.

Brian then asked if there were any ways for a Nazi to evade the GR reasoning. I told him that Hare had sketched several escape strategies, but that none were very satisfactory. Let me give four of these:

1. The Nazi could use "ought" in a way that doesn't express a universalizable prescription. Then he could reject the GR consistency condition.

In this case, the Nazi's use of "ought" would be peculiar and misleading. He'd do better to avoid moral language and just say that he *wants* to mistreat Jews.

2. The Nazi could refuse to make moral judgments on the issue.

Then we couldn't refute his moral views, because he doesn't have any. We can't beat him at the game of morality if he doesn't play the game. Note that our consistency condition applies only if you make an ought judgment about how you ought to treat the other person.

3. The Nazi could say that he doesn't care about being inconsistent and irrational.

Then he's admitted that we've refuted him.

4. The Nazi could desire that he and his family be put in concentration camps and killed if they were Jewish.

Such a Nazi could be consistent. But only a crazy person would have such desires.

So the GR argument is strong, but not inescapable. The argument becomes decisive for a person who wants to make genuine moral judgments on the case (1 and 2) in a consistent way (3) and doesn't have crazy desires (4). Thus prescriptivism gives a strong way to reason. With most other views, we can't argue further when we run into a difference on a basic moral principle. Prescriptivism goes further because it appeals to consistency.

Let me sum up my approach to moral rationality. To think rationally about ethics is to think in a way that is informed, imaginative, and consistent. And the most important part of consistency is to follow the golden rule.

Before going to Section 6.5, reflect on your initial reaction to prescriptivism. What do you like or dislike about the view? Do you have any objections?

6.5 Objections

Ima's approach to ethics has many virtues. It does a fine job in showing how moral thinking can be both free and rational. It gives a brilliant analysis of the golden rule. And it gives useful tools for reasoning about moral issues. While its approach to moral rationality resembles that of the ideal observer view (see Chapter 2), it works out the details more clearly and adds a powerful consistency component. The most questionable part of the view, however, seems to be its analysis of "ought."

Ima's view divides into two parts:

(1) *Rules of moral reasoning:* To be logically consistent, we must make similar evaluations about similar cases, live in harmony with our moral beliefs, and follow the golden rule.
(2) *Analysis of "ought":* Ought judgments are universalizable prescriptions – not truth claims.

Some critics object to formulating (1) in terms of *logical consistency*. They say that we commit no logical inconsistency if we make conflicting judgments about similar cases, violate our moral beliefs, or violate the golden rule. Some of these critics think that the so-called *logical rules* in (1) are better seen as very general *moral rules*:

(1a) We *ought* to make similar evaluations about similar cases, live in harmony with our moral beliefs, and follow the golden rule.

The logical rules in (1) are based on the analysis of "ought" in (2). But this analysis has further problems, since it implies that ought judgments aren't truth claims, and so aren't literally true or false. This seems to conflict with how we approach ethics in our daily lives.

When we deliberate about a moral issue, we generally assume that there's a truth of the matter that we're trying to discover. We're not just trying to develop rational desires; we're also trying to discover the truth about how we ought to live. And we speak as if there are moral truths. We use words like "true," "false," "correct," "mistaken," "know," and "discover" of moral judgments – but not of imperatives. When we use such objective language, we can't plausibly substitute a universalizable prescription for an ought judgment. Suppose that I say this:

(a)   I know that *you ought to do this.*

Prescriptivism claims that the italicized part is a universalizable pre-scription, and means "Do this and let everyone do the same in similar cases." But we can't substitute the latter for the former:

(b)   I know that *do this and let everyone do the same in similar cases.*

Here (a) makes sense but (b) doesn't. So prescriptivism seems to clash with how we use moral language.

Ima could reply that our moral practice is wrong when it speaks of moral knowledge and moral truths. Or he could accept these notions, but water them down; maybe calling an ought judgment "true" just endorses the judgment (and doesn't make an objective claim). While these responses are possible, the presumption seems to lie with our moral practice. If so, then we should accept moral truths and moral knowledge unless we have strong arguments to the contrary.

Ima says it doesn't matter that moral judgments aren't true or false. What matters is that we can refute Nazi racists and teach our children to think rationally about moral issues. Prescriptivism does a good job on these. For example, it gives powerful ways to show that Hitler's moral beliefs were irrational – even though these beliefs weren't literally false. Prescriptivism gives strong moral arguments, but not moral truths. But I'd like to have both. I'd like to use GR reasoning to discover moral truths – for example, that Hitler's moral beliefs were false.

Ima's rejection of moral truths makes it easier for Nazis to escape the GR argument. Ima's consistency conditions tell us what we have to do, *if* we choose to use "ought" consistently. But we might avoid using "ought." If we do so, we don't violate any moral truths and don't violate GR consistency. On Ima's view, none of these is a moral truth:

- We ought to make moral judgments about our actions.
- We ought to be consistent.
- We ought to follow the golden rule.

Moral truths would make it more difficult to escape the GR argument.

Where do we go from here? We might try to combine ideas from intuitionism and prescriptivism – so we'd have both moral truths and strong ways of reasoning about morality. Or we might try to develop prescriptivism's tools of moral reasoning in a neutral way that could be defended from various views on the foundations of ethics. We'll work on both ideas in the next three chapters.

6.6 Chapter summary

Prescriptivism sees moral judgments as a type of prescription, or imperative. Moral judgments, like the simple imperative "Close the door," don't state facts and aren't true or false. Instead, they express our will, or our desires.

Ought judgments are universalizable prescriptions. "You ought to do this" is equivalent to "Do this and let everyone do the same in similar cases." So moral beliefs express our desire that a kind of act be done in the present case and in all similar cases – including ones where we imagine ourselves in someone else's place.

Prescriptivism shows how can we be both free and rational in forming our moral beliefs. Moral beliefs can be *free* because they express our desires and aren't provable from facts. They can be *rational* because the logic of "ought" leads to a method of moral reasoning that engages our rational powers to their limits.

Moral beliefs are subject to two basic logical rules:

U. To be logically consistent, we must make similar evaluations about similar cases.
P. To be logically consistent, we must keep our moral beliefs in harmony with how we live and want others to live.

Rule U holds because moral judgments are universalizable: it's part of their meaning that they apply to similar cases. Rule P holds because moral judgments are prescriptions (imperatives), and thus express our will, or our desires, about how we and others are to live.

Prescriptivism's GR consistency condition, which follows from these two logical rules, claims that this combination is inconsistent:

• I believe that I ought to do something to another.
• I don't desire that this be done to me in the same situation.

This consistency condition is a more precise version of the traditional golden rule ("Treat others as you want to be treated"). We violate it if we think we ought to do something to another, but don't desire that this be done to us in the same situation.

To think rationally about ethics, we need to be informed, imaginative, and consistent; the most important part of consistency is to follow the golden rule. This approach can show that Nazi moral beliefs are irrational – since Nazis wouldn't be consistent in their moral beliefs if they knew the facts of the case and exercised their imagination.

Prescriptivism, while it has important insights, seems to rest on a questionable foundation. It says that ought judgments are universalizable prescriptions (or imperatives), and not truth claims. This leads it to deny the possibility of moral knowledge and moral truths – which seems to conflict with how we approach ethics in our daily lives.

6.7   Study questions

Write out the answers in your ethics folder. If you don't know an answer, go back to the section that deals with it.

1. How does prescriptivism define "ought"? What method does it follow for arriving at moral beliefs?
2. What is a "prescription"? What does it mean to say that ought judgments are "universalizable" prescriptions?
3. How do imperatives differ from indicatives? (6.1)
4. Did Ima reject the idea of moral truths? Did this make his view "just like emotivism"?
5. Are imperatives necessarily emotional? Give some examples to show that imperatives can be highly rational.
6. Explain what Ima said about moral freedom and rationality. (6.2)
7. What was Brian's problem? What did he want from Ima?
8. How is the meaning of "ought" the key to how we can be both free and rational in our moral thinking?
9. What are the two logical rules about moral consistency? What are they based on? (6.3)
10. Explain the golden rule consistency condition. Does it say how we ought to live?
11. Explain (using the example of stealing Detra's bicycle) how the GR consistency condition follows from the idea that moral judgments are universalizable prescriptions.
12. What three elements do we need in order to think rationally about ethics?
13. How did Ima answer Brian's question? How did he say that we can reason about basic moral principles? (6.4)

14. How did Ima argue against Nazi moral beliefs? In what four ways could Nazis evade the GR reasoning?
15. Write about a page sketching your initial reaction to prescriptivism. Does it seem plausible to you? What do you like and dislike about it? Can you think of any way to show that it's false?
16. What do some critics say about prescriptivism's consistency rules?
17. Explain the objection to Ima's analysis of "ought." How might Ima reply to this objection? (6.5)
18. How does the rejection of moral truths make it easier for Nazis to escape the golden rule reasoning?

6.8 For further study

To solidify your understanding, do the computer exercises for "Ethics 06 – Prescriptivism." Also do review exercises "Ethics 06r," "Ethics 06v," and "Ethics 06z." The Computer Exercises appendix at the end of this book has further information on this and on Internet resources.

For more on prescriptivism, see Hare's *Freedom and Reason*; I especially recommend Chapters 1, 6, and 11. His earlier *The Language of Morals* focuses on imperatives and moral language; his later *Moral Thinking* defends utilitarianism. For some technical criticisms of Hare's approach, see Section 6.5 of Gensler's *Formal Ethics*. The Bibliography at the end of the book has information on how to find these works.

CHAPTER 7
Consistency

CHAPTER 7
Consistency

Avoid inconsistencies between:

- your beliefs (logicality),
- your ends and means (ends–means consistency),
- your moral judgments and how you live (conscientiousness), and
- your evaluations of similar actions (impartiality).

Our next three chapters sketch a practical approach to moral rationality. Since the approach stresses consistency and the golden rule, I call it the "GR consistency view." It develops tools of moral reasoning that practically any ethical theory could use.

This chapter gives four basic consistency principles. The following two chapters discuss the golden rule and other elements of moral rationality. The resulting moral methodology resembles that of prescriptivism, except that it's developed further and doesn't rest on a prescriptivist analysis of moral terms.

7.1 Avoiding an impasse

How should we select a method for picking out our moral principles? The usual approach is to build on what we take moral judgments to mean. So we follow a religious method if we take moral judgments to be about God's will; we get other methods if we take them to be about social conventions, personal feelings, or independent objective truths. The problem here is that people continue to disagree on how to understand moral judgments. This would seem to lead to a permanent impasse (or stalemate) on how to reason about morality.

I'd like to suggest a way out of the difficulty. There may be consistency principles that give powerful tools for moral reasoning and that make sense from various perspectives. I have in mind principles like "Be logically consistent in your beliefs," "Follow your conscience," "Make similar evaluations about similar cases," and "Treat others as you want to be treated." These ideas are already widely accepted. Here we need to formulate them more clearly, see how to use them in moral reasoning, and show how to defend them from various perspectives (as self-evident truths, God's will, social conventions, or whatever). So this chapter will examine four basic consistency principles.

Here's a parallel. Most of the principles of math and logic are clear and uncontroversial. Few would dispute claims like "x+y = y+x" or "If all As are Bs, and all Bs are Cs, then all As are Cs." But the basis for such principles is disputed. Are they true because of language conventions? Or do they express independent, objective truths? Or did God make them true? Or are they empirical? Philosophers disagree on these foundational questions; but they accept much the same principles of math and logic. Maybe moral consistency principles can work the same way. Maybe these too can be widely shared tools for moral reasoning, even though people disagree about their ultimate basis.

7.2 Consistency in beliefs

Logicality is the requirement that we be logically consistent in our beliefs. We violate this if we accept incompatible beliefs – or if we accept a belief without also accepting its logical consequences.

Suppose that Ima Relativist begins her philosophy paper like this:

> Since morality is relative, no duties bind universally. What's right in one culture is wrong in another. Universal duties are a myth. Relativism should make us tolerant toward others; we can't say that we're right and they're wrong. So everyone ought to respect the values of others.

Here Ima's first statement is incompatible with her last:

- No duties bind universally.
- Everyone ought to respect the values of others.

If *everyone* ought to respect the values of others, then some duties bind universally. And if *no* duties bind universally, then neither does the duty to respect others. Ima's views are deeply confused and inconsistent. This often happens when we first try to formulate our philosophical views.

Logicality forbids inconsistent belief combinations. Consistency would require that Ima give up one belief or the other of her inconsistent pair.

But it doesn't tell her which one to give up. This is an important feature of consistency principles: they forbid inconsistent combinations but don't tell us specifically what to believe or what to do.

Logicality also requires that we accept the logical consequences of our beliefs. Suppose that we accept a principle, but then someone points out its implausible consequences. Do we accept these consequences? If we accept a principle but reject its consequences, then we're inconsistent – and we have to change something. Thus we can argue about first principles by appealing to consistency. Later we'll see how this can be useful in attacking racist arguments and principles.

Here's a more formal statement of the logicality requirement:

If A and B are logically inconsistent with each other, then don't combine these two: • I believe A. • I believe B.	If A logically entails B, then don't combine these two: • I believe A. • I don't believe B.

These use "don't combine." We also could say "we *ought* not to combine." I'll assume that we *ought* to be consistent; later in this chapter we'll discuss *why* we ought to be consistent.

Let me end this section by answering some questions about logicality.

(Q1) Does logicality tell us to prove all our beliefs?

No, it only requires that our beliefs be consistent with each other. We can't prove all our beliefs, since this would require an infinite chain of arguments, where each premise is proved by some further argument.

(Q2) Does logicality tell us to shun emotions?

No, it only requires that we be consistent. This has little to do with how emotional we are. Some highly emotional people have consistent belief systems, while some unemotional people have inconsistent beliefs.

(Q3) Is logicality about metaethics or about normative ethics?

It's about both. Since it tells us that we *ought* to be consistent in our beliefs, it's part of normative ethics. Since it gives us a condition that we need to fulfill to be *rational* in our moral beliefs, it's also part of metaethics. All our consistency conditions have this dual aspect.

(Q4) Does the consistency duty have exceptions?

Yes. It wouldn't apply, for example, if we're psychologically unable to be consistent (perhaps because of some mental defect) or if some stronger duty interferes (perhaps Dr Evil will destroy the world unless we're inconsistent in some minor way). All our consistency duties are subject to implicit qualifications (see Gensler 1996: 15–39).

(Q5) Does consistency guarantee truth?

No. We might be consistent but wrong. However, consistency often points us toward the truth. Suppose that you murder your roommate and then make up a story to cover your tracks. If a clever detective investigates and questions you, you'll find it hard to keep your story consistent. Uncovering inconsistencies may be the best way to discover the truth about the murder. So consistency, while not guaranteeing truth, can point us toward the truth.

7.3   Consistency in will

Besides inconsistency in beliefs, there's also inconsistency in will. This leads to two further consistency requirements: ends–means consistency and conscientiousness.

Ends–means consistency is the requirement that we keep our means in harmony with our ends. I violate this if (a) I have an end, (b) I believe that to fulfill this end I need to carry out certain means, and (c) I don't carry through on the means. For example:

- I want to lose weight.
- I believe that to lose weight I need to eat less or exercise more.
- I don't eat less or exercise more.

If I combine these three, then consistency requires that I change something – that I give up my goal, or my belief, or that I follow through on the means.

Ends–means inconsistency, like inconsistency in beliefs, is common. We humans have a strong tendency to do what's easy or what brings immediate satisfaction (like eat a big desert), instead of what's needed to fulfill our deeper goals. Aristotle defined a "human" as a "rational animal"; but we're imperfectly rational, and our rational and animal dimensions can struggle against each other.

Inconsistency of will also can occur in other ways. For example, I might make a firm resolution (to run every day), but then act against it (I keep putting it off and don't do it). Or I might have goals (to become a doctor and to party all the time) that I realize are incompatible. Or I might violate conscientiousness.

Conscientiousness is the requirement that we keep our actions, resolutions, and desires in harmony with our moral beliefs. We violate this if our moral beliefs clash with how we live and want others to live.

Suppose that I hold the pacifist belief that one ought never to kill a human being for any reason. If I'm conscientious, then (a) I'll never intentionally kill a human being myself, (b) I'll be resolved not to kill for any reason (even to protect my life or the lives of my family), and (c) I won't want others to kill for any reason.

While my pacifist example is about an "ought" belief, similar requirements cover beliefs about what is "all right" ("permissible"). If I'm conscientious, then I won't believe that something is *all right* without consenting to (approving of) the idea of it being done. And I won't do something without believing that it would be *all right* for me to do it.

Expressed as an imperative, conscientiousness says "Avoid inconsistencies between your moral judgments and how you live." Here's a more specific conscientiousness imperative:

Don't combine these two:

- I believe that I ought to do A now.
- I don't do A now.

If we combine these (as we often do), then our moral belief clashes with how we live – and consistency requires that we change one or the other.

"We ought to follow our conscience" could be taken in two ways:

1. We ought to avoid inconsistencies between our moral beliefs and our actions.
2. Our conscience is always correct: if we believe that we ought to do something, then this is really what we ought to do.

The second interpretation has bizarre implications. It entails "If we believe that we ought to commit mass murder, then this is really what we ought to do." The first interpretation, which follows our approach, is better. It simply forbids an inconsistency between our beliefs and our actions. If the two clash, then something is wrong with one or the other.

Here's a consistency analogue of "Practice what you preach":

> Don't combine these two:
>
> - I believe that everyone ought to do A.
> - I don't do A myself.

This is a specific case of the general requirement to avoid inconsistencies. It doesn't presume that our principles are correct – so that if we preach universal hatred then it becomes our duty to hate. Instead, it tells us to avoid inconsistencies between our principles and our actions. If the two clash, then something is wrong with one or the other.

I've spoken of conscientiousness as a type of "consistency" between our moral beliefs and our lives. I'm leaving it open whether to take this "consistency" in the specific sense of "logical consistency," or in the more generic sense of "agreement" (or "harmony").

Suppose that my moral beliefs conflict with how I live. Prescriptivism says that I then violate logical consistency (since I'm misusing the term "ought"). Other views might say that I violate a conscientiousness duty – a duty to keep my life in harmony with my moral beliefs; this duty might rest on a social convention, a personal ideal, a divine command, or a self-evident truth. On these views, violating conscientiousness would involve an objectionable clash between my moral beliefs and how I live, but not necessarily a logical inconsistency or self-contradiction.

Consistency is often useful in attacking flawed moral principles. Suppose that I accept the principle, "All short people ought to be beat up – just because they're short." My principle commits me to other things:

> If I hold this: ➔ All short people ought to be beat up – just because they're short.
>
> Then, to be consistent, I must *believe* that if I were short then I *ought* to be beat up.
>
> And I must *desire* that if I were short then I be beat up.

If I don't believe and desire these things, then I'm inconsistent and my moral thinking is flawed.

7.4 Racist arguments

To see further how to use consistency, let's imagine that we're disputing with Ima Racist, who holds that all blacks ought to be treated poorly. Here "treat X poorly" is a shorthand description that might be filled in differently for different sorts of racism – as, for example, "enslave X" or "insult X and keep X in low-paying jobs."

Ima Racist tells us, "Blacks ought to be treated poorly, because they're inferior." How do we respond to his argument? Should we dispute his factual premise, and say "All races are genetically equal"? Or should we counter with our own moral principle, and say "People of all races ought to be treated equally"? Either strategy will likely lead to a stalemate, where Ima has his premises and we have ours, and neither side can convince the other.

I suggest instead that we formulate Ima's argument clearly and then watch it explode in his face. Ima's conclusion, presumably, is about how *all* blacks ought to be treated. So his premise needs to say that *all* blacks are inferior. And he needs another premise that *all* inferior people ought to be treated poorly. His argument then goes this way:

> All blacks are inferior.
> All who are inferior ought to be
> treated poorly.
> ∴ All blacks ought to be treated poorly.

To clarify this further, we need to find out what Ima means by "inferior." What puts someone into the "inferior" group? Is it IQ, or education, or wealth, or physical strength, or what? Let's suppose that Ima decides on an IQ criterion. For him, let us suppose, "inferior" = "of IQ less than 80." Then his argument goes:

> All blacks have an IQ of less than 80.
> All who have an IQ of less than 80
> ought to be treated poorly.
> ∴ All blacks ought to be treated poorly.

Once he assigns this meaning to "inferior," it becomes clear that his inferior/non-inferior division cuts across racial lines. Every race has some members with an IQ of less than 80, and some with an IQ of greater than 80. So the first premise is clearly false. And we can remind Ima that his second premise also applies to whites:

> All who have an IQ of less than 80
> ought to be treated poorly.
> ∴ All *whites* who have an IQ of less
> than 80 ought to be treated poorly.

To be consistent, Ima must believe that he ought to treat low-IQ whites poorly (as he treats blacks). And he has to treat these whites poorly himself, and desire that others do so too. As a racist, Ima will reject these consequences of his principle. So he'll be inconsistent. To restore consistency, he must either give up his principle or else accept its consequences about whites.

Our strategy for criticizing racist arguments has three steps:

1. Formulate the argument. The premises must be clearly stated, and the conclusion must clearly follow from the premises.
2. Criticize the factual premises if necessary.
3. See if the racist applies his moral premise consistently, especially to his own race.

If the racist's conclusion is about how *all* blacks (or Jews) are to be treated, then he needs a criterion to separate the races cleanly, so all blacks will be on one side and all whites on the other. An IQ number doesn't do this – and neither does any other plausible criterion. These considerations of logic and consistency will destroy most racist arguments. (For further considerations, see Gensler 1996: 158–65.)

Suppose that Ima gives up his "inferiority" *argument*, but still wants to treat blacks poorly. He now claims that the mere difference in skin color merits a difference in treatment. So he insists on the *principle*: "All blacks ought to be treated poorly, just because of their skin color."

Again, we can appeal to consistency. Does Ima consistently discriminate by skin color? He'd have to treat albino blacks well (since they have light skin), while he'd treat poorly any whites who have deep, dark tans. And if someone invented a cosmetic called *Skin So Pale* that turned black skin permanently white, he'd have to discriminate only against blacks who didn't use it.

Ima also would have to desire that if he and his family were black then they'd be treated poorly. To dramatize the idea, we could tell him Hare's (1963: 218) delightful story about the color-changing germ that is about to infect the world. The germ turns originally white skin permanently black and originally black skin permanently white. Does Ima really desire that if this happened then the newly white people be treated well, and the newly black people (including himself and his family) be treated poorly? With questions like these, we can show Ima that his moral thinking is inconsistent and thus flawed.

Appealing to consistency is often useful in moral disputes. The appeal is powerful, since it doesn't presume material moral premises (which the other party may reject) but just points out problems in someone's belief system. But at times, of course, consistency won't do the job by itself and we need other ways to carry the argument further.

Let me distinguish between racist arguments, principles, and actions:

1. *Argument:* "Blacks are inferior and inferior people ought to be treated poorly; therefore, blacks ought to be treated poorly."
2. *Principle:* "Blacks ought to be treated poorly, just because they're black."
3. *Actions:* Ima treats blacks poorly.

So far, we know how to use consistency to attack the first two, but not the third. We haven't yet talked about how to use consistency against a racist who won't defend his actions in a principled way. We'll return to this problem later, in Chapter 9.

7.5 Impartiality

Impartiality is the requirement that we make similar evaluations about similar actions, regardless of the individuals involved. If we're impartial, then we'll evaluate an act based on what the act is like – and not based on who plays what role in the situation. If we judge that an act is right (or wrong) for one person to do, then we'll judge that the same act would be right (or wrong) for anyone else to do in the same situation.

I violate impartiality if I make conflicting evaluations about actions that I regard as *exactly similar* or *relevantly similar*. Two actions are **exactly similar** if they have all the same properties in common. They are **relevantly similar** if the reasons why one fits in a given moral category (good, bad, right, wrong, or whatever) also apply to the other.

In the actual world, no two actions are ever *exactly similar* (have *all* the same properties in common). But the notion applies usefully to hypothetical cases. To test my impartiality, I can imagine an *exactly similar* action in which the parties are in different places – in which, for example, I am on the receiving end of the action.

Here's an example adapted from the Good Samaritan parable (Luke 10:30–5). Suppose that, while I'm jogging, I see a man who's been beaten, robbed, and left to die. Should I help him, perhaps by running back to make a phone call? I think of excuses why I shouldn't. I'm busy, don't want to get involved, and so on. I say to myself, "It would be all right for me not to help him." But then I consider an exactly reversed situation. I imagine myself in his place; I'm the one who's been beaten, robbed, and left to die. And I imagine him being in my place; he's jogging and sees me in my sad state. I ask myself, "Would it be all right for this man not to help me in this situation? Surely not!" But then I'm inconsistent. What is all right for me to do to another has to be all right for the other to do to me in an imagined exactly reversed situation.

In the actual world, no two acts are exactly similar. But we can always *imagine* an exactly similar act. If I'm about to do something to another, I can *imagine* what it would be like for this to be done to me in an exactly similar situation. I violate impartiality if I combine these two beliefs:

- It would be *all right* for me to do such and such to X.
- In an exactly similar situation, it would be *wrong* for X to do this to me.

This sounds like the golden rule. But it's really about impartiality, since it deals with making similar *evaluations* about similar actions; it deals with beliefs about right and wrong. The genuine golden rule of the next chapter is about *actions* and *desires* ("*Treat others* as you *want to be treated*"), not about evaluations.

My Good Samaritan example refers to an imagined "exactly reversed situation" in which all my properties are switched with those of the other person. Let me explain this idea further. Suppose that we list my properties and those of the other person (X):

My properties: jogging very busy has blue eyes ...	*X's properties:* beaten and robbed needs a doctor has brown eyes ...

Imagine that the list contains all our properties, even complex ones. The list would be too long to write out – perhaps infinitely long. When I imagine an *exactly reversed situation*, I imagine a situation where the list of properties is reversed:

My properties:	X's properties:
beaten and robbed	jogging
needs a doctor	very busy
has brown eyes ...	has blue eyes ...

Here I'm beaten and robbed, and X is the jogger. We also have to reverse relationships. So if X helped me in the past, then in the reversed situation I'd imagine that I helped X in the past.

Instead of switching *all* the properties in my mind, I could switch just the ones relevant to evaluating the act. If I'm not sure if a property is relevant, I could switch it anyway – just to be on the safe side. This approach has me imagine a "relevantly similar" reversed situation.

Here's another example. I'm driving and see a hitchhiker. Should I pick him up? If I don't, he may spend a long and frustrating time waiting; I know what this is like from when I've hitchhiked to backpacking trails. On the other hand, people who pick up hitchhikers are sometimes robbed or hurt. Impartiality tells me that whatever judgment I make on my-picking-up-the-hitchhiker (that it's obligatory, or wrong, or neutral), I must make the same judgment on the imagined reversed situation act. Impartiality doesn't tell me what to do; and here it doesn't push me toward an obvious answer. Rather, it encourages me to reflect on the act from both perspectives (mine and the hitchhiker's). And it emphasizes that, whatever I decide, I must apply the same standards to myself that I apply to others.

These examples test our impartiality by seeing how we evaluate an *imagined* second case. The following example uses an *actual* second case that's recognized to be relevantly similar. This example also shows how this sort of reasoning can help us to recognize duties toward ourselves.

In the movie *Babe*, the athlete Babe Didrikson Zaharias (1914–56) needed a colostomy operation to save her life. Out of fear, she decided that she shouldn't have it. But her husband, thinking that she should have it, had her talk with another woman in similar circumstances, who also had to choose between dying and having the operation. Babe instinctively told the woman, "You ought to take courage and have the operation – for life is the greatest gift there is." But then Babe realized that she had to apply the same principles to herself that she applied to others. So she decided that she too ought to have the operation.

Let's consider the case more carefully. Babe combined three beliefs:

(a)   I ought not to have the operation.
(b)   You ought to have the operation.
(c)   Our cases are relevantly similar.

She held (a) because she feared the results of the operation, she held (b) because of the value of life ("the greatest gift there is"), and she held (c) because she thought that any reasons that would justify one operation would justify the other. She saw that her beliefs were inconsistent and that she had to change something. She could reject (a), (b), or (c). She in fact rejected (a), saying that she too ought to have the operation, just as the other woman in her similar situation should have it. She could have rejected (b), saying that neither should have the operation; she didn't do this, because she so strongly believed that the other woman ought to have it. Or she could have rejected (c), saying that the operation was right in one case but not the other, because of such and such differences; she didn't do this, because she couldn't think of any reason that would justify one operation but not the other. So consistency, while not telling her what to believe, helped her to form her beliefs.

Consistency norms respect our moral freedom, since they don't tell us specifically what to do or what to believe. At the same time, they promote the rationality of ethics, since they guide us on how to work out our views in a consistent way.

I've spoken of impartiality as a type of "consistency" between our evaluations. I'm leaving it open whether to take this in the specific sense of "logical consistency," or in the more generic sense of "uniformity."

Suppose that I make conflicting evaluations about similar actions. Prescriptivism says that I then violate logical consistency (since I'm misusing the term "ought"). Other views might say that I violate an impartiality duty – a duty to make similar evaluations about similar actions; this duty might rest on a social convention, a personal ideal, a divine command, or a self-evident truth. On these views, violating impartiality would involve an objectionable clash between my moral evaluations, but not necessarily a logical inconsistency or self-contradiction.

Let me end this section by raising some questions about impartiality. Remember that, as we're taking the term, *impartiality* requires that we make similar evaluations about actions that we take to be exactly or relevantly similar.

(Q1) Do we violate impartiality if we say "It's *all right* for you to drive but *wrong* for your brother to drive?"

No. We might point out differences between the cases (for example, that you have a license but he doesn't) that we take to justify the difference in evaluations. Impartiality must include a clause about the acts being relevantly or exactly similar.

(Q2) Does impartiality require that we treat everyone the same way?

No. We might give extra help to someone who requires it (as in the Good Samaritan case). This needn't involve making conflicting evaluations about similar actions.

(Q3) Does impartiality require that we love everyone equally?

No. It would destroy friendships and families if we had to love everyone equally. Suppose that we love our children more that we love strangers – and we think that it would be all right for *any parent* in similar cases to do the same thing. Then we're making similar evaluations about similar actions, and we satisfy impartiality.

(Q4) Does impartiality require that we always act the same way in the same kind of situation?

No. Life would be very boring if we had to do this. Suppose that we have a Coke one time, and then later in a similar situation have a Pepsi. We might regard both actions as neutral (all right either to do or to omit doing) – and thus evaluate them the same way. Remember that we only violate impartiality (as I use the term) if we make conflicting *evaluations* about actions that we regard as relevantly or exactly similar.

(Q5) Isn't the appeal to *relevantly similar* actions slippery? What prevents me from appealing to trivial differences? Suppose that I'm the only person with six toes. What keeps me from saying, "It's all right for me to kill you, but wrong for you to kill me, because I have six toes and you don't"?

If you pick trivial differences, we can defeat you by appealing to a hypothetical case. Imagine a case where I have six toes (instead of you). Do you really think that in this case it would be all right for me to kill you? No one would believe this.

In appealing to relevant differences between cases, we have to be factually accurate (that the factor applies in one case but not the other) and consistent (giving the factor equal weight regardless of which side is imagined to have it). These conditions aren't so easy to satisfy.

At times, though, the appeal to *relevantly similar* cases can get slippery. It's often cleaner to appeal to imagined *exactly similar* cases.

7.6 Why be consistent?

We've proposed four consistency norms: logicality, ends–means, conscientiousness, and impartiality. These norms would get very wide (but perhaps not universal) support from thinkers of very different perspectives. These thinkers, however, may accept the consistency norms for quite different reasons. To dramatize this, I'll let my Ima characters explain why they endorse consistency.

Ima Relativist: "I accept all four consistency norms as social conventions. These norms are needed for a society to function and so are accepted by practically every society."

Ima Subjectivist: "I accept the consistency norms because they fit my feelings. I'm an idealistic person, and thus am emotionally attracted to being impartial, conscientious, and so forth. And I welcome these norms, since they add a rational structure to my subjectivist view.

"When I'm in my selfish mood, as I sometimes am, I can justify consistency by appealing to self-interest. I note that:

1. Inconsistency leads to confusion and the frustration of our desires. To see this, imagine how miserable our lives would be if whenever we believed (or wanted) something we also believed (or wanted) the opposite thing. We'd go crazy!

2. Inconsistency is inherently painful; psychologists speak here of *cognitive dissonance*. Perhaps evolution programmed our minds to avoid inconsistencies, as it programmed our bodies to spit out many poisons.

3. Inconsistency brings social penalties. It cuts us off from rational discussion, since it leads people to dismiss our ideas. Society is especially harsh on us when we violate conscientiousness or impartiality; it trains us to feel guilt, anxiety, and the loss of self-respect in these cases.

For these reasons, self-interest supports consistency."

Ima Emotivist: "I accept the consistency norms because they accord with my feelings. I agree fully with Ima Subjectivist."

Ima Idealist: "I support consistency because it's an important part of being rational. And I'd like to add that an 'ideal observer' must be consistent in the ways sketched in this chapter."

Ima Supernaturalist: "Inconsistency is bad because God is against it. The Bible often condemns inconsistency. For example, Jesus (in Luke 13:14–17) criticized hypocritical Pharisees whose actions clashed with their words. The Bible says much to support conscientiousness and impartiality."

Ima Prescriptivist: "We're logically inconsistent when we violate conscientiousness or impartiality, since we're misusing the term 'ought.' My view presupposes that we *ought* to be logically consistent. I see this, not as a truth, but as an imperative that we choose to live by."

Ima Intuitionist: "Consistency is the first duty of a rational being. In any area of thought, inconsistency is a defect. The consistency duty is a self-evident truth. It's immediately obvious, and further investigations reveal no absurd implications.

"The duty to be consistent can't be proved by any truth that's more basic. That consistency is socially approved (or promotes your self-interest, or whatever) doesn't show that it's right. Every argument presupposes the value of consistency (since the essence of valid reasoning is that accepting the premises forces you, under pain of inconsistency, to accepting the conclusion). So if you don't already see the value of consistency, then I'm wasting my time if I try to reason with you. So we can't argue for the value of consistency without circularity.

"People object that moral principles are vague and widely disputed, and hence can't be self-evident. But the consistency norm is precise and widely held. In fact, you can't do science or mathematics without it. So I see no reason to deny that it's a basic self-evident truth."

I'll assume our consistency norms in the chapters that follow; but I won't assume any particular way to defend them. I myself agree with Ima Intuitionist's defense. For the reasons given in Chapter 4, I think that "good" is indefinable and that there are objective moral truths. I differ from classical intuitionism in that I accept only one basic self-evident moral truth – namely, that we ought to be consistent (in the ways sketched in this chapter). The rest of ethics can be derived from this in ways that I'll sketch in the next two chapters.

7.7   Chapter summary

How should we reason about ethics? There seems to be a permanent impasse (or stalemate) on this, since people continue to disagree on how to understand moral judgments.

I'd like to suggest a way out of the difficulty. There may be moral consistency principles that give powerful tools for moral reasoning and that make sense from various perspectives. We'll develop this idea in this chapter and the next two. We'll start with four basic consistency requirements: logicality, ends–means consistency, conscientiousness, and impartiality.

Logicality says "Avoid inconsistent beliefs." I violate this if I accept incompatible beliefs – or if I accept a belief without also accepting its logical consequences.

Ends–means consistency says "Keep your means in harmony with your ends." I violate this if (a) I have an end, (b) I believe that to fulfill this end I need to carry out certain means, and (c) I don't carry through on the means.

Conscientiousness says "Keep your actions, resolutions, and desires in harmony with your moral beliefs." This forbids inconsistencies between my moral judgments and how I live.

Consistency can be useful in arguing about ethics – for example, in arguing against a racist who says that blacks ought to be treated poorly because they're inferior. Our strategy for criticizing racist arguments has three steps: (1) Formulate the argument. The premises must be clearly stated, and the conclusion must clearly follow from the premises. (2) Criticize the factual premises if necessary. (3) See if the racist applies his moral premise consistently, especially to his own race.

Impartiality says "Make similar evaluations about similar actions, regardless of the individuals involved." I violate this if I make conflicting evaluations about actions that I regard as exactly or relevantly similar. To test my impartiality, it can be useful to ask whether I'd make the same evaluation about a similar case in which the parties are in different places – in which, for example, I'm on the receiving end of the action.

We could base these consistency norms on practically any approach to ethics. For example, we might see them as based on social conventions, personal feelings, self-interest, God's will, or self-evident truths.

7.8 Study questions

Write out the answers in your ethics folder. If you don't know an answer, go back to the section that deals with it.

1. What is the usual approach to selecting a method for picking out moral principles? Why does it lead to an impasse? (7.1)
2. What solution is suggested for arriving at ways of reasoning about ethics? How will these ways of reasoning be justified?
3. Do philosophers accept roughly the same principles of math and logic? Do they justify these principles the same way?
4. What is logicality? In what two ways could we violate it? (7.2)
5. Explain the example about Ima Relativist.
6. Does consistency guarantee truth? If not, then of what use is it?
7. What is the ends–means consistency requirement? Give a concrete example of how we might violate it. (7.3)
8. What is the conscientiousness requirement? How would a conscientious pacifist live?
9. Explain two ways to take "You ought to follow your conscience."
10. How could we use consistency to argue against the principle that all short people ought to be beat up?
11. How could we criticize Ima Racist's argument: "Blacks ought to be treated poorly – because they're inferior"? Explain the three steps for criticizing racist arguments. (7.4)
12. How could we criticize Ima's principle: "All blacks ought to be treated poorly, just because of their skin color"?
13. Explain the impartiality requirement. What does it mean to call two acts "exactly similar" and "relevantly similar"? (7.5)
14. Explain the Good Samaritan example and how it illustrates one way to test our impartiality.
15. Explain the example about Babe and her operation.
16. Give two misinterpretations of impartiality and explain why they are wrong.
17. How could we criticize a person who says: "It's all right for me to kill you, but wrong for you to kill me, because I have six toes and you don't"?
18. How might one defend consistency using cultural relativism, subjectivism, supernaturalism, and intuitionism? (7.6)
19. How might one defend consistency by self-interest?

7.9 For further study

To solidify your understanding, do the computer exercises for "Ethics 07 – Consistency." The Computer Exercises appendix at the end of this book has further information on this and on Internet resources.

This chapter is a condensed and simplified version of Chapters 1 to 4 of Gensler's *Formal Ethics*; see this for further details and references. Gensler's "Ethics is based on rationality" had an earlier version of the view. Many of the ideas were inspired by Hare's *Freedom and Reason* and Kant's *Groundwork of the Metaphysics of Morals*. The Bibliography at the end of the book has information on how to find these works.

CHAPTER 8
The Golden Rule

CHAPTER 8
The Golden Rule

GR Theorem:	GR forbids this combination:
Treat others only as you consent to being treated in the same situation.	• I do something to another. • I'm unwilling that this be done to me in the same situation.

The golden rule requires that we treat others only as we consent to being treated in the same situation. GR is the most important principle in this book, and perhaps the most important rule of life. This chapter is about GR.

GR can be derived from the consistency requirements of our previous chapter. So this chapter builds on previous ideas. Applying GR requires further elements, like knowledge and imagination, that we'll discuss in the following chapter.

8.1   A GR theorem

Our GR theorem is expressed in two ways at the top of the page. To apply GR, you'd imagine yourself in the other person's place on the receiving end of the action. If you act in a given way toward another, and yet are unwilling to be treated that way in the same situation, then you violate the rule.

Here's an example. President Kennedy appealed to the golden rule in an anti-segregation speech during the first black enrollment at the University of Alabama. He asked whites to consider what it would be like to be treated as second-class citizens because of skin color. They were to imagine themselves being black – and being told that because of this they couldn't vote, go to the best public schools, eat at most public restaurants, or sit in the front of the bus. Would whites be content to be treated that way? He was sure that they wouldn't; yet this is how they treated others. He said the "heart of the question is whether we are going to treat our fellow Americans as we want to be treated."

To apply the golden rule, we need to *know* what effect our actions have on the lives of others. And we need to *imagine* ourselves, vividly and accurately, in the other person's place on the receiving end of the action. When combined with knowledge and imagination, GR is a powerful tool of moral thinking.

GR is a consistency principle. It doesn't replace regular moral norms. It isn't an infallible guide on what is right or wrong. It only prescribes consistency – that we not have our actions (toward another) be out of harmony with our desires (about a reversed-situation action).

GR follows from conscientiousness and impartiality. Suppose that you want to steal Detra's bicycle. And suppose that you're conscientious (keep your actions and desires in harmony with your moral beliefs) and impartial (make similar evaluations about similar actions). Then you won't steal her bicycle unless you're also willing that your bicycle be stolen in the same situation. This chart shows the steps in the derivation:

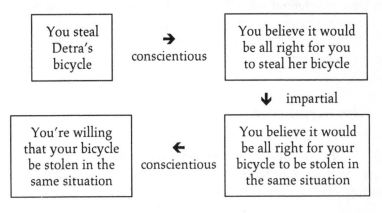

Here's a less graphical version of the argument. If we're conscientious and impartial, then:

> We won't do something to another unless we believe that this act would be all right.
> We won't believe that this act would be all right unless we believe that it would be all right for this to be done to us in the same situation.
> We won't believe that it would be all right for this to be done to us in the same situation unless we're willing that this be done to us in the same situation.
> ∴ We won't do something to another unless we're willing that this be done to us in the same situation.

So if we're conscientious and impartial, then we'll follow GR: we won't do something to another unless we're willing that it be done to us in the same situation. But we've been assuming (see Chapter 7) that we *ought* to be conscientious and impartial. It follows that we *ought* to follow GR: we *ought* to treat others only as we consent to being treated in the same situation.

So our GR isn't a basic principle. Instead, it's provable from the conscientiousness and impartiality requirements. Our GR is a *theorem* – something provable from principles that are more basic.

Let's compare our GR with prescriptivism's GR (see Section 6.3) – which also holds on our approach:

> *Prescriptivism's GR* says that this combination is inconsistent: (a) I believe that I *ought* to do something to another, and (b) I don't desire that this be done to me in the same situation.

Our GR is stronger in three ways. First, we can violate it even if we don't use "ought"; so we can't escape it by refusing to make moral judgments. Second, we can defend our GR using practically any approach to ethics; so it doesn't assume a controversial prescriptivist analysis of moral terms. Third, views that accept moral truths could accept that our GR expresses an important moral truth about how we ought to live.

8.2 The literal rule

People usually formulate the golden rule in simple ways, like "Treat others as you want to be treated." If we take this formulation literally, we get the literal golden rule (LR):

> **Literal Golden Rule (LR):**
>
> If you want X to do something to you, then do this same thing to X.

LR has no same-situation clause and tells what specific act to do (instead of forbidding an action–desire combination).

LR often works well. Suppose that you want Suzy to be kind to you; then LR tells you to be kind to her. Or suppose that you want Tom not to hurt you (or rob you, or be selfish to you); then LR tells you not to do these things to him. These applications seem sensible. But LR can lead to absurdities in two ways. First, there are cases where you are in *different circumstances* from X:

- To a patient: If you want the doctor to remove your appendix, then remove the doctor's appendix.
- To a violent little boy who loves to fight: If you want your sister to fight with you, then fight with her.
- To a parent: If you want your child not to punish you, then don't punish him.

Second, there are cases where you have *defective desires* about how you are to be treated:

- To a masochist who wants to be tortured: If you want X to torture you, then torture X.

LR leads to absurdities because its wording is defective.

GR's same-situation clause avoids the first kind of objection. Consider this case. I speak loudly to my father (who is hard of hearing); but I don't want him to speak loudly to me (since my hearing is normal). While this is sensible, it violates LR. LR says that if I want my father to speak normally (not loudly) to me, then this is how I am to speak to him. LR ignores differences in circumstances. LR tells me: "If you want others to treat you in a given way in your present situation, then this is how you are to treat them – even if their situation is very different."

With GR, I'd ask how I desire that I'd be treated if I were in the *same situation* as my father (and thus hard of hearing). I desire that if I were in his same situation then people would speak loudly to me. So I'd speak loudly to him.

We can take "same situation" here as "exactly similar situation" or "relevantly similar situation." In the first case, I'd imagine myself in my father's *exact place* (with all his properties). In the second, I'd imagine myself having those properties of my father (such as being hard of hearing) that I think are or might be *relevant* to deciding how loudly one should speak to him. Either approach works fine.

The same-situation clause is also important for the appendix case. Recall that LR told the patient to remove the doctor's appendix. The same-situation clause would block this, since the patient clearly doesn't desire that if he were in the place of his doctor (with a healthy appendix), then his appendix be removed by a sick patient ignorant of medicine. In applying GR, we need to ask, "Am I willing that the same thing be done to me *in the same situation?*"

In the fighting case, LR told the violent little boy to fight with his sister. The same-situation clause would block this. The little boy should imagine himself in the place of his sister (who is terrorized by fighting) and ask "Am I willing that I be fought with in this way if I were in her place?" Since the answer is "no," he wouldn't fight with his sister.

We need to be careful about something else. GR is about our present reaction to a hypothetical case. It isn't about how we would react if we were in the hypothetical case itself. We have to ask the right question:

Ask this	➜	Am I willing that this be done to me in the same situation?
Not this	➜	If I were in the same situation, would I then be willing that this be done to me?

The difference here is important, but subtle. Let me try to clarify it.

Suppose that I have a two-year-old son, little Will, who keeps putting his fingers into electrical outlets. I try to discourage him from doing this, but nothing works. Finally, I decide that I need to spank him when he does it. I want to see if I can spank him without violating GR. I should ask the first question – not the second:

Good form: Am I now willing that if I were in Will's place then I be spanked?	This has "willing that if." It's about my present adult desire toward a hypothetical case.

Bad form: If I were in Will's place, would I then be willing to be spanked?	This has "if" before "willing." It's about the desires I'd have as a small child.

With the *good form*, I imagine the case in the following box:

THE GOLDEN RULE 109

> I'm a two-year-old child. I put my fingers into electrical outlets, and the only way to discourage me from doing this is through a spanking. Of course, I know nothing about electricity and I desire not to be spanked.

As an adult, I say "I *now* desire that if I were in this situation then I be spanked." I might add, "I'm thankful that my parents spanked me in such cases – even though I wasn't pleased then." Thus I can spank my child without breaking GR – since I'm willing that I would have been treated the same way in the same situation.

On the other hand, if I were in Will's situation, and thus judged things from a two-year-old mentality, then I'd desire not to be spanked. That's what the **bad form** is about. If we formulated GR in terms of this, then I'd break GR if I spanked Will. But this is absurd. We need to formulate GR using the **good form**, in terms of my present reaction to a hypothetical case. I can satisfy GR because I'm now (as an adult) willing that I would have been spanked in this situation.

This point is subtle, but of central importance. If you don't get the idea, I suggest that you reread the last few paragraphs a few times until it comes through.

This distinction is crucial when we deal with someone who isn't very rational – such as a person who is in a coma, or who is senile or confused. We need to ask the right question:

Ask this	➔	How do I *now* desire that I'd be treated if I were in a coma?
Not this	➔	If I were in a coma, how would I *then* desire to be treated?

GR is about our *present* attitude toward a hypothetical case. To use GR correctly, say "I DESIRE THAT IF"; don't say "WOULD DESIRE."

Let me sum up where we are. Recall that the literal golden rule LR can lead to absurdities in two ways. First, there are cases where you are in *different circumstances* from the other person. We can get around these by including a same-situation clause and being careful to ask the right question. Second, there are cases where you have *defective desires* about how you are to be treated. LR can tell a person with defective desires to do evil things. For example, it can tell a masochist who wants to be tortured to torture another; we'll consider this example in the next section. Here we'll consider a simpler case that shows why we need to take GR, not as a direct guide to action, but rather as prescribing consistency between our actions (toward another) and our desires (about a reversed-situation action).

Imagine this case. We own a very profitable coal mine, but act wrongly in paying our workers only a miserly $1 a day. People ask if we're willing to be paid $1 a day in their place. We answer "yes," and thus are consistent. But we answer "yes" only because we think (incorrectly) that our workers can live tolerably on this amount. If we knew the truth, we wouldn't answer "yes." So here we're consistent and follow GR, but only because we're ignorant.

Here we satisfy GR-consistency but act wrongly. This shows that we shouldn't take GR to be an infallible guide on what is right or wrong. Properly understood, GR doesn't tell us what specific action to do. Instead, it forbids inconsistent combinations.

GR gives us a useful tool for attacking certain inconsistencies. But here we need something else. We need to correct our view of the facts. Only then can GR show us our error in how much we pay our workers.

Our GR formulation has three key features:

- a *same-situation* clause,
- a *present attitude* toward a hypothetical situation, and
- a *don't-combine* form.

We need these features to avoid absurd implications and to insure that GR is derivable from conscientiousness and impartiality.

8.3 Masochists

The literal golden rule LR can tell a person with defective desires to do evil things. For example, it can tell a masochist who wants to be tortured to torture another:

- If you want X to torture you, then torture X.

This is the most difficult objection to the golden rule. But now we have at least some of the tools needed to handle the objection.

In dealing with masochist cases, we need a three-fold attack:

1. We need to have the masochist imagine himself in the other person's place.
2. We need to recall that GR forbids an inconsistent action–desire combination – and doesn't tell us what specific act to do.
3. We need some way to criticize irrational desires.

We'll develop point 3 about irrational desires in the next chapter.

Suppose that Ima Masochist is considering whether to torture a nonmasochist X. To apply GR, Ima should ask:

> "Am I willing that I be tortured if I were in the exact place of X (who is a nonmasochist)?"

If Ima is a typical masochist, he'll answer "no." Typical masochists desire physical or emotional pains because these bring sexual, athletic, or religious satisfactions. Ima wouldn't get these satisfactions if he were in the place of X (a nonmasochist). So to be tortured in X's place would be sheer agony. To answer "yes" to the question, Ima would have to be an unusual masochist. He'd have to hate himself so much that he desires that he be tortured even if he were in the place of a nonmasochist. But let's suppose that Ima hates himself in this way – and so answers "yes."

Would GR then command that Ima torture X? The answer is "no," since GR doesn't command specific actions. Instead, it forbids inconsistent combinations:

GR forbids this **→** inconsistent combination	• I do something to another. • I'm unwilling that this be done to me in the same situation.

Since GR only forbids inconsistencies, it doesn't tell Ima to torture X. And it doesn't assume that our desires about how we are to be treated are perfectly fine and give us a flawless guide on how to treat others.

But GR has a weakness. Suppose that Ima tortures another and is willing to be tortured in the same situation; then he satisfies GR consistency. So we can follow GR and still act wrongly. In general, this doesn't discredit a principle. Consider "One ought not to lie." We can follow this and still act wrongly – since we might torture or kill, instead of lying.

Our coal-mine case also showed that we can be consistent and follow GR, but still act wrongly. This can happen, for example, if we're ignorant about how our actions affect others, or if our desires are defective. So consistency isn't enough. GR gives a useful tool for attacking defective attitudes on the basis of consistency. But we may also need other tools of criticism.

Perhaps we can show Ima that his desires are defective. Recall that he'd have to have a strong self-hatred to desire that he be tortured if he were in the place of a nonmasochist. We could counter Ima's self-hatred by getting him to understand himself better (including the source of his hatred), appreciate his self-worth, and experience positive ways of living. If he developed a love for himself, then GR could extend this love-of-self to love-of-others. So GR may not suffice *by itself* to show Ima his error. But it may suffice when combined with other factors.

In the next chapter, we'll say more about how to criticize desires – especially racist desires. My main point here is that GR is useful in many cases and doesn't imply absurdities. GR forbids a common kind of inconsistency. In the few cases where one could follow GR while acting wrongly, this may come from taking GR in isolation. GR works best when combined with other factors, such as knowledge, imagination, and rationalized desires.

8.4   GR questions

(Q1) Is the golden rule widely accepted?

Yes. Many endorse GR and put it at the heart of their moral thinking. For example, professionals often use GR to explain their responsibilities toward others. So a thoughtful nurse might say, "I try to treat my patients as I'd want to be treated in their place." Many in education, business, or government say similar things.

The golden rule has wide support among the various religions and cultures of the world. Jesus Christ, Confucius, and the Rabbi Hillel all used the rule to summarize their teachings. Buddhism, Hinduism, Islam, Taoism, and Zoroastrianism also support GR, as do secular thinkers from diverse cultures. Many of these give the rule a central status in moral thinking. GR is close to being a global principle – a norm common to all peoples of all times.

The golden rule, with roots in a wide range of world cultures, is well suited to be a standard that different cultures can appeal to in resolving conflicts. As the world becomes more and more a single interacting global community, the need for such a common standard is becoming more urgent.

(Q2) How does GR relate to "Love your neighbor"?

"Love your neighbor" tells us to have concern for others. This means that we are to seek to do good and not harm to them – and to do this for their own sake. "Love your neighbor" specifies a motivation. If we *love* others, then we're motivated to care about others for their own sake.

GR and "Love your neighbor" are more complementary than equivalent. Love is the highest motive for following GR (which we also might follow for lower motives like self-interest). If we follow GR out of love, then we follow it because we care about others for their own sake.

GR, in turn, gives a workable way to operationalize the somewhat vague idea of "loving your neighbor." To love your neighbor in the GR way, follow these three steps:

1. Know your neighbor as well as you can.
2. Imagine yourself in the place of your neighbor, as vividly and accurately as you can.
3. Act toward your neighbor only in ways in which you're willing to be treated in the same situation.

If you love your children in the GR way, for example, you'll make a great effort to know and understand them (including their needs and desires). You'll put yourself in their place and try to imagine what their lives are like for them. And you'll treat them only in ways that you're willing to be treated yourself by a parent in the same situation.

(Q3) Is the golden rule the summary of all morality?

This depends on how we take the question. Are we looking for a single principle that always, when combined with factual premises, tells us what specific act we ought to do? Our GR won't do this. Forms that directly guide action, like the literal golden rule, can lead to absurdities when we have defective desires.

Properly interpreted, the golden rule doesn't say what specific act to do. Instead, it forbids inconsistent action–desire combinations. Thus GR doesn't compete with principles like "It's wrong to steal" or "One ought to do whatever maximizes enjoyment." GR operates at a different level.

The golden rule captures the *spirit* behind morality. It helps us to see the point behind moral rules. It engages our reasoning, instead of imposing an answer. It counteracts self-centeredness. And it concretely applies ideals like fairness and concern. So GR makes a good one-sentence summary of what morality is about.

(Q4) Is GR the same as "Treat others as they treat you"?

No, although the two are often confused. "Treat others as they treat you" tells you to do good to those who do good to you – and to harm those who harm you. This can lead to revenge and retaliation.

Young children, when they learn the golden rule, often misunderstand it to say "Treat others as they treat you. If someone hits you, then hit him back." They regard this approach as fair. Wiser people see that this leads to endless revenge – and so they prefer the golden rule.

(Q5) Isn't the GR theorem too subtle and difficult for normal people to understand?

It does have subtle aspects. We need these to avoid the objections and to show that the golden rule is defensible. Less sophisticated people can always fall back on the very simple literal golden rule.

(Q6) Suppose you live in a ruthless "dog eat dog" society, where everyone takes advantage of everyone else. Wouldn't people take advantage of you if you followed the golden rule?

Not necessarily. GR permits self-defense. You can defend yourself against the attacks of evil people in ways that you consent to others defending themselves against you in a similar case. So you can eat the other dog (who tries to eat you) if you consent to your being eaten in a similar case (where you try to eat another). Even in a dog-eat-dog world, however, GR would limit how harshly we could treat others. And it may lead us to work toward a better society in which everyone follows GR.

(Q7) What is the scope of the golden rule? Does it apply just to human beings – or perhaps just to our tribe or group? Does it apply to animals or things?

GR says that you [agent] are to treat another [recipient] only as you consent to being treated in the same situation. So there are two questions. First, what *agents* does "you" apply to? Second, what *recipients* does "another" apply to?

First, GR governs the actions of *rational agents*. GR forbids inconsistent action–desire combinations. GR wouldn't apply to beings who can't act intentionally or can't consent to hypothetical actions.

Second, GR deals with how to treat *sentient recipients* – beings capable of experiences (past, present, or future). GR is vacuous when we apply it to nonsentient objects. Consider this instance of GR (which leaves unspecified what kind of being X is):

> Don't step on X without consenting to the idea of your being
> stepped on if you were in X's exact place.

We can derive this instance from the general duties to be conscientious
(to live in harmony with our moral beliefs) and impartial (to make
similar evaluations about similar actions); neither of these duties is
restricted to how we treat *humans*. The instance works normally if X is a
sentient being – like a friend, a stranger, or a dog. I care about whether I
be stepped on if I were in the place of any of these, since then being
stepped on would hurt me. But the instance is vacuous for practical
purposes if X is a rock or other nonsentient being. I don't care about
whether I be stepped on if I were in the place of a rock. Rocks feel no
pain. So I step freely on rocks – but not on friends, strangers, or dogs.

Consider this GR instance about torturing your dog:

> Don't torture your dog without consenting to the idea of your
> being tortured if you were in your dog's place.

This works like GR as applied to humans. Of course, it's more difficult to
understand what it's like to be a dog, and to imagine yourself in the
dog's place. Those who deal with canines may find this easier; but this
example doesn't demand a subtle knowledge of dogs. So I see no reason
not to apply GR to animals.

I'm reminded of a traditional African proverb: "One who is going to
take a pointed stick to pinch a baby bird should first try it on himself to
feel how it hurts." This suggests that we are to apply GR to baby birds
and to all other sentient creatures.

> (Q8) GR helps us to see our duties toward others. Are there
> any similar principles that can help us to see our duties toward
> ourselves?

Yes. We violate consistency if we treat others as we aren't willing to
be treated. But we also violate consistency if we treat *ourselves* as we
aren't willing to have *others* treat *themselves*. This is the **self-regard
principle**. To use it effectively, we must imagine someone we care about
acting as we propose to act.

Here are some examples. Maybe you have so much concern for your
children that you never think of your own needs; but you aren't willing
that your children live in a similar way when they grow up. Or you go
through college without putting much effort into it; but you don't
consent to the idea of a daughter of yours doing this in the same situation. Or, because you lack courage and a sense of self-worth, you refuse

to seek treatment for a drug habit that's ruining your life; but you aren't willing that your younger brother do this in a similar situation. In all these cases, you're inconsistent and violate self-regard.

We tend to think of people as too selfish and too little concerned for others. But people often don't have much concern for themselves either. Various factors (laziness, fear, habit, lack of self-appreciation, lack of discipline, and so forth) can drive us into ways of living that benefit neither ourselves nor others. Our consistency requirements recognize the importance of both concern for others and concern for ourselves.

GR and the self-regard principle imaginatively shift the *persons* in the situation. But we also can shift the *time* – and imagine that we *now* experience the future consequences of our actions. We violate consistency if we treat ourselves (in the future) as we aren't willing to have been treated by ourselves (in the past). This is the **future-regard principle**. More crudely: "Don't do what you'll later regret."

Here are some examples. Maybe you cause yourself a future hangover by your drinking; but, when you imagine yourself experiencing the hangover *now*, you don't consent to the idea of your having treated yourself this way. Or you cause yourself a future jail sentence by stealing; but when you picture yourself suffering these consequences *now* because of your past actions, you don't consent to these actions. In both cases, you're inconsistent and violate future-regard.

> (Q9) The golden rule is about your treatment of X. What if your action affects two others, X and Y?

I must satisfy the golden rule toward both. Suppose that I own a small store and need to hire just one worker. X and Y apply, and I have to choose between them. Both are qualified, but X more than Y. The one I don't pick will be disappointed. To make a choice consistently, I must be willing for anyone to make that choice in that situation – regardless of which place in the situation I imagine myself in. So if I pick X (who is more qualified) instead of Y, then I have to be willing that I *not* be picked if I were in Y's situation.

The **formula of universal law** expresses this idea more elegantly:

Formula of Universal Law:

Act only as you're willing for anyone to act in the same situation – regardless of imagined variations of time or person.

These "imagined variations" include cases where you're in the place of someone affected by your action (GR), where someone you care about is in your place (self-regard), or where you're at a future time experiencing the consequences of your action (future-regard). The formula of universal law is a generalization of the golden rule; it also includes the self-regard and future-regard ideas.

My "formula of universal law" is named after a famous (but somewhat different) formula of the eighteenth-century philosopher Immanuel Kant. In many ways, my GR consistency view is a contemporary restatement of Kant's approach to ethics.

(Q10) Could you sum up your consistency principles?

Our last chapter specified *four basic* consistency principles:

- Logicality: Avoid inconsistent beliefs.
- Ends–means: Keep your means in harmony with your ends.
- Conscientiousness: Keep your actions, resolutions, and desires in harmony with your moral beliefs.
- Impartiality: Make similar evaluations about similar actions, regardless of the individuals involved.

This present chapter presented *four derivative* principles:

- Golden rule: Treat others only as you consent to being treated in the same situation.
- Self-regard: Treat yourself only as you're willing to have others treat themselves in the same situation.
- Future-regard: Treat yourself (in the future) only as you're willing to have been treated by yourself (in the past).
- Universal law: Act only as you're willing for anyone to act in the same situation – regardless of imagined variations of time or person.

My student Elizabeth Murphy suggests that we remember these by thinking of CELI FUGS (pronounced "silly fugs"). She says that fugs are little creatures that don't practice conscientiousness, ends–means, logicality, and impartiality (CELI) – or future-regard, universal law, golden rule, and self-regard (FUGS). That's why they're silly.

8.5 Why follow GR?

This section is redundant, since GR follows from consistency duties that we already defended. However, some views support GR more firmly and directly than how they support consistency in general. And GR is so important that it's useful to see how it fits into different approaches to ethics. So I'll now let the Ima characters explain why they endorse GR.

Ima Relativist: "I accept the golden rule as a social convention. Practically every society accepts GR – since this rule helps us to resolve social conflicts in a way that people find acceptable. A society without GR (or something equivalent) wouldn't survive very long."

Ima Subjectivist: "I accept GR because it fits my feelings. I'm an idealistic person, and thus care about people for their own sake. And I feel that the world would be a better place if we all followed GR. So I have an emotional attraction toward GR.

"When I'm in my selfish mood, as I sometimes am, I can justify following GR by appealing to self-interest. I note that:

1. Following GR promotes cooperation – which benefits everyone (including myself). Selfishness promotes conflict – which ultimately hurts everyone (including myself).
2. People mostly treat us as we treat them. So it generally pays in terms of self-interest to treat others well.
3. Violating GR brings penalties – including social disapproval and alienation from others. And society trains us to feel guilt and lose self-respect when we violate GR.
4. Following GR makes us feel good about ourselves and brings us the respect and admiration of others.

So self-interest can justify GR fairly well.

"Some people think that intelligent crooks might promote their self-interest better by only *pretending* to follow GR. But this strategy usually fails. Most crooks are caught, or live in the fear of being caught, and end up living very unsatisfying lives.

"An experiment by Rimland 1982 gives further evidence that self-interest supports GR. Many groups were asked to list the persons that they knew best, and then label them as 'happy' or 'unhappy,' and as 'altruistic' or 'selfish.' When the responses are analyzed, 'happy' people are almost always 'altruistic' and almost never 'selfish.' So, judging by people's perceptions, self-interest seems to support GR."

Ima Emotivist: "I accept the golden rule because it accords with my feelings. I agree fully with Ima Subjectivist."

Ima Idealist: "I support GR because it's required by consistency and hence by rationality. And I'd like to add to my definition of 'ideal observer' that such a being would follow GR."

Ima Supernaturalist: "We ought to follow the golden rule because it's God's law. Christianity endorses GR (see Matthew 7:12 and Luke 6:31), as do all the other major world religions. We are all brothers and sisters, created by a loving Father, a God who wants us to love one another and follow the golden rule."

Ima Prescriptivist: "I see GR as built into our moral language. And I choose to use moral language, and thus follow GR, because I value the kind of life, for myself and for others, that this leads to."

Ima Intuitionist: "Our GR is a self-evident truth – a known truth that requires no further proof or justification. Almost everyone will see its correctness right away; and further investigations uncover no absurd consequences.

"Of course, our GR *can* be proven by more basic consistency require-ments. This is useful to do, as a way of organizing our moral consistency principles into a system. But the principle is clearly true in itself – even without such a proof."

I myself agree with Ima Intuitionist.

8.6 Chapter summary

Our golden rule theorem says: "Treat others only as you consent to being treated in the same situation." To apply GR, I'd imagine myself in the other person's place on the receiving end of the action. GR forbids this combination: (a) I do something to another, and yet (b) I'm unwill-ing that this be done to me in the same situation.

GR doesn't tell us what specific act to do. And it doesn't replace regu-lar moral norms. It only prescribes consistency – that we not have our actions (toward another) be out of harmony with our desires (about a reversed-situation action). To apply GR adequately, we need knowledge and imagination.

If we're conscientious and impartial, then we'll follow GR – since then we won't do something to another unless we believe it would be all right – and thus believe it would be all right to do to us in the same situation – and thus are willing that it be done to us in the same situation.

The literal GR says: "If you want X to do something to you, then do this same thing to X." This can lead to absurdities if we are in different circumstances from X or if we have defective desires about how we are to be treated. To avoid these, our GR uses a same-situation clause, a present attitude toward a hypothetical situation, and a don't-combine form.

The golden rule is close to being a global principle – a norm common to all peoples of all times. It makes a good summary of morality and a good way to operationalize the idea of "loving your neighbor." Closely related to GR are the self-regard and future-regard principles, and the formula of universal law: "Act only as you're willing for anyone to act in the same situation – regardless of imagined variations of time or person."

We could base the golden rule on practically any approach to ethics. For example, we might base GR on social conventions, personal feelings, self-interest, God's will, or self-evident truths.

8.7 Study questions

Write out the answers in your ethics folder. If you don't know an answer, go back to the section that deals with it.

1. Give the two formulations of the golden rule theorem.
2. Explain Kennedy's use of the golden rule. What two further factors do we need to apply GR? (8.1)
3. Explain, using the example about stealing Detra's bicycle, how GR follows from conscientiousness and impartiality.
4. In what three ways does our GR theorem differ from prescriptivism's GR?
5. What is the literal GR? Give some objections to it. (8.2)
6. Explain the "hard of hearing" case – and how our GR formulation deals with it.
7. Explain the "punishing your child" case – and how our GR formulation deals with it. What do we have to be careful about here?
8. A murderer tells the judge: "If you were in my place, you wouldn't want to be sent to jail. Hence by the golden rule you can't send me to jail." Show how this uses the "bad form." How could the judge answer using the "good form"?
9. Could we follow GR and yet still act wrongly? Use the "coal mine" example in your answer.
10. What are the three key features of our GR formulation?
11. Explain the "masochist" objection to the golden rule – and how our view deals with it. (8.3)
12. How widely accepted is the golden rule? (8.4)

13. What motivation would "Love your neighbor" give to GR? What three steps does GR use to operationalize "love your neighbor"?
14. Children sometimes interpret GR as saying "Treat others as they treat you." How does this formula differ from the golden rule?
15. In a dog-eat-dog world, would people who follow GR necessarily be taken advantage of?
16. What is GR's scope? Does GR apply to our treatment of animals?
17. Explain the self-regard and future-regard principles.
18. How does GR apply if your action affects two other parties? What is the formula of universal law?
19. What does "CELI FUGS" stand for?
20. How might one defend GR using cultural relativism, subjectivism, supernaturalism, and intuitionism? (8.5)
21. How might one defend GR by self-interest?

8.8 For further study

To solidify your understanding, do the computer exercises for "Ethics 08 – The Golden Rule." The Computer Exercises appendix at the end of this book has further information on this and on Internet resources.

This chapter is a condensed and simplified version of Chapters 5 and 6 of Gensler's *Formal Ethics*; see this book for further details and references. Wattles's *The Golden Rule* is a fine book-length discussion of GR, focusing on historical and religious aspects. For shorter discussions, see Hertzler's "On golden rules," Singer's "The golden rule," and Cadoux's "The implications of the golden rule." Many of the ideas in this chapter were inspired by Hare's *Freedom and Reason* and Kant's *Groundwork of the Metaphysics of Morals*. The Bibliography at the end of the book has information on how to find these works.

CHAPTER 9
Moral Rationality

Moral Rationality

Moral Rationality:

We're rational in our moral judgments to the extent that we're consistent, informed, imaginative, and a few more things.

How can we pick out our moral principles in the wisest and most rational way? How can we reason and argue about moral issues? What does moral rationality require?

The last two chapters gave part of the answer. Moral rationality requires consistency, which includes the golden rule. But rationality also requires other elements, like knowledge and imagination. We now need to complete the picture.

9.1   Rationality conditions

I suggest that we're more rational in our moral thinking to the extent that we're more (1) consistent, (2) informed, (3) imaginative, and (4) a few more things. While we'll never be completely rational, we can strive for greater rationality.

(1) *Consistent.* We need to be *consistent* in the ways that we've sketched in the last two chapters. These include logicality, ends–means consistency, conscientiousness, impartiality, the golden rule, self-regard, future-regard, and the formula of universal law.

(2) *Informed.* As far as possible, we need to know the situation, alternative moral views, and ourselves.

First, we need to know the situation: circumstances, alternatives, consequences, and so on. To the extent that we're misinformed or ignorant, our thinking is flawed. (An exception to this is that it may be desirable to eliminate information that may bias or cause cognitive overload.)

Second, we need to know alternative moral views, including arguments for or against them. Our thinking is less rational if we're unaware of opposing views.

Finally, we need self-knowledge. By understanding our biases, we can to some extent neutralize them; so we need to know how our feelings and moral beliefs originated. For example, some people are hostile toward a group because they were taught this when they were young. Their attitudes might change if they understood the source of their hostility and broadened their experience. If so, then their attitudes are less rational – since they exist because of ignorance.

Of course, we can never know *all* the facts; and we often must act quickly and have no time to research a problem. But we can act out of greater or lesser knowledge. Other things being equal, a more informed judgment is a more rational one.

(3) *Imaginative.* As far as possible, we need a vivid and accurate awareness of what it would be like to be in the place of those affected by our actions. This differs from just knowing facts. So in dealing with poor people, besides knowing facts about them, we also need to appreciate and envision what these facts mean to their lives. Movies, literature, and personal experience can help us to visualize another's life.

Imagining another's perspective is a common human experience. A child pretends to be a mother or a soldier. A chess player asks, "If I were in my opponent's place, how would I respond to this move?" A writer dialogues with an imagined reader who misunderstands and raises objections. A teacher asks, "How would I respond to this assignment if I were a student?" The ability to take another's perspective (empathy) is especially important for applying the golden rule.

We also need to appreciate the future consequences of our actions on ourselves. Knowing that drugs have harmful effects differs from being able to imagine these effects in a vivid and accurate way. An essay about drug addiction might give us the facts, while a story or movie about drug addicts might bring these facts to life for us.

(4) *A few more things.* Here are five additional suggestions (Gensler 1996: 151–2 has a longer list):

- Feel free to think for yourself (instead of just conforming).
- Develop feelings that support the rational principles – especially feelings of concern for yourself and for others. Feelings can guide us when we don't have time to think things out.
- Dialogue with others in your society and in other societies. Other people can point out our inconsistencies and make us aware of factors to which we'd otherwise be blind.

- In areas where you don't have the time or ability to be very rational, give weight to the views of those who are more rational – especially if there's a consensus.
- Don't be dogmatic on areas where rational people differ.

Keep in mind that many of our rationality conditions are idealized and that only God could satisfy them completely.

Our rationality conditions link up in various ways. Ends–means rationality requires that we harmonize our ends and our means; but it's also about understanding our goals, how they originated, and how to achieve them. Impartiality requires that we make similar evaluations about similar actions; but it's also about taking account of facts and arguments on both sides of an issue. Concern for others relates to the golden rule; but it's also about understanding others, imagining ourselves in their place, and having feelings of concern.

We're *rational* in our moral beliefs to the extent that in holding them we satisfy the rationality conditions – and thus are consistent, informed, imaginative, and a few more things. This gives a criterion, not of what is "true," but of what is "rational." Someone might satisfy the rationality conditions to a high degree but still have moral beliefs that are incorrect. This wouldn't disprove our principles.

Our **rationality conditions** are principles stating how we *ought* (ideally) to form our moral beliefs. Most of our conditions aren't very controversial. But we can still ask *why* we should follow these conditions and not others. How can we *justify* our rationality conditions?

The short answer is that these rationality conditions grow out of the consistency requirements that we've already defended. Consider the "Be informed" condition. Since we demand that others try to be informed when they deliberate about how to act toward us, we will, if consistent, demand this of ourselves too – and hold that we and others *ought* to be so informed. So consistency will lead us to accept "Be informed" as a rationality condition. In a similar way, consistency will lead us to accept "Be imaginative" and the other conditions.

Since our rationality conditions are ought judgments, their status is controversial. Are they objective, irreducible truths about how we ought to do our moral thinking? Are they demands of society, of ideal observers, or of God? Or are they exclamations or imperatives, instead of truths? People will disagree on the *status* of the conditions; but they may still largely agree on their *content*. Indeed, I think that the most plausible content is much the same, regardless of how we view the nature of moral judgments.

9.2   Rational desires

We noted earlier that golden-rule reasoning can be less effective if
people have flawed desires about how they are to be treated. People may
then satisfy GR consistency and yet act wrongly. Recall:

- the Nazi of Section 6.4, who desires (out of hatred for Jews)
  that he and his family be put in concentration camps and
  killed if they were found out to be Jewish.
- the coal-mine owner of Section 8.2, who is willing (since he's
  ignorant of the cost of things) that he be paid only a miserly
  $1 a day if he were in the place of his workers.
- the masochist of Section 8.3, who desires (out of self-hatred)
  that he be tortured if he were in the place of a non-masochist.

For golden-rule reasoning to work properly, we need some way to
criticize such desires. We suggested that the desires of the coal-mine
owner and of the masochist are irrational if they came from ignorance
and would be given up if the person understood things correctly.

We can use the rationality conditions of the previous section to criticize desires. Irrational desires have flaws like inconsistency, ignorance,
or lack of imagination. Our desires might be:

- inconsistent with our actions, other desires, or moral beliefs.
- based on *current* false beliefs. Maybe our desire to become a
  doctor rests on false beliefs about our abilities.
- based on *previous* false beliefs. Maybe we avoid yogurt only
  because we once believed it was poisonous. Our desire to avoid
  yogurt remains, even though we gave up this false belief.
- based on a faulty generalization. Maybe we avoid a certain
  group because of non-typical personal experiences. But this
  would change if we broadened our experiences.
- based on social conditioning. Maybe we avoid a certain group
  because we were taught to do so. But our desire would change
  if we understood this and broadened our experiences.
- based on lack of imagination. Maybe we'd give up our desire
  to be a doctor if we imagined the life of a doctor more vividly
  and accurately.

So our desires might be irrational for various reasons.

My favorite example of an irrational desire used to be my father's
desire not to eat yogurt. His desire came from misinformation ("Yogurt
contains bad germs"), his association of yogurt with weird people (his

children), and his anti-yogurt upbringing. But he later broadened his knowledge and experience, and changed his desires. Now he eats yogurt.

My current favorite example is my own desire not to eat worms. My desire is irrational because it's based on social conditioning and would diminish or disappear if I broadened my knowledge and experience. I know that my society conditioned me to shudder at the idea of eating worms – even though worms can be prepared in healthy and appetizing ways, are easy to farm, and are a delicacy in some cultures. But I lack experience. Some day I may visit a distant land and enjoy a delicious *ver de terre* (earthworm) meat loaf. With an openness to new experiences, I could change my irrational desire not to eat worms.

My anti-worm desire is trivial. But it isn't trivial when people are conditioned to hate those of another group. It's important that socially taught desires can be rationally criticized. To apply GR adequately may involve rationally criticizing our desires – as we'll see in the next section.

9.3   GR and racism

Applying GR to racism will show how our view on rationality applies to an important issue. As before, I'll imagine that we're arguing with Ima Racist, who defends extreme racist policies like Nazism, South African apartheid, or Southern slavery or segregation. I'll use "treat X poorly" as a shorthand description that might be filled in differently – for example, as "enslave X" or "insult X and keep X in low-paying jobs." In Section 7.4, we distinguished between racist arguments, principles, and actions – and showed how to demolish the first two:

1.   *Argument:* "Blacks are inferior and inferior people ought to be treated poorly; therefore, blacks ought to be treated poorly."
2.   *Principle:* "Blacks ought to be treated poorly, just because they're black."
3.   *Actions:* Ima treats blacks poorly.

Now we have the ammunition to mount a GR attack against someone who performs racist actions but won't defend his actions in a principled way.

Before going into details, I note that various people in pro-slavery societies have used GR reasoning to conclude that slavery is wrong. Historical examples include the stoic philosopher Epictetus in 90, the Pennsylvania Quakers in 1688, and Harriet Beecher Stowe and Abraham Lincoln in the 1800s. (Gensler 1996: 147 has references.)

Our GR attack on racist actions has four steps:

1. Get Ima to understand the facts. In particular, have him understand how his actions affect people of the other race.
2. Get Ima to imagine himself, vividly and accurately, in the place of his victims, on the receiving end of the action.
3. If needed, try to make Ima's desires (about how he be treated in the place of his victims) as rational as possible.
4. If Ima acts in a given way toward those of another race, but doesn't consent to himself being treated that way in the same situation, then he's inconsistent and violates GR.

Don't go to the golden rule (step 4) too quickly. GR builds on understanding, imagination, and desires – each of which may be flawed. After working on these, we can apply GR more rationally and effectively.

Step 1 is to get Ima to understand the facts – circumstances, alternatives, consequences, and so on. When Kennedy applied GR to racism, he first tried to get whites to understand what segregation was doing to black people. Blacks were treated as second-class citizens because of skin color. They couldn't vote, go to the best public schools, eat at most public restaurants, or sit in the front of the bus. These practices brought further poverty, frustration, and a decreased sense of self-worth.

We can learn about another's situation by observation and testimony. So we might have Ima *observe* blacks – how they live and how segregation affects them. And we might have him listen to the *testimony* of blacks about how they are treated.

Step 2 tries to get Ima to realize the *human significance* of the facts. Ima needs a vivid and accurate awareness of the situation of blacks, and what it would be like to be in that situation. Accordingly, he might read a novel or watch a movie that portrays their lives. Or he might act out the role of a person who is discriminated against. Or he might relive, in his imagination, cases where he himself was treated poorly because of his background. Or he might just explore in his imagination what it would be like to receive such treatment.

Step 4 involves applying the golden rule. If we sense that steps 1 and 2 have prepared Ima sufficiently, we might ask him:

> Now you can better understand the situation of blacks and imagine what it would be like to be treated as you treat them.
> Do you consent to the idea of yourself and your family being treated this way in their place?

Ima likely won't consent to this; so he'll likely be inconsistent and violate GR. But let's suppose that he consents to himself being treated as a second-class citizen in their place, and thus satisfies GR. This only could happen if he has a disinterested hatred for blacks and thus desires that all blacks suffer – including himself and his family if they were black (or were found to have black ancestry).

Such hatred is possible. There's a story about a Nazi who hated Jews and put them in concentration camps. One day he discovered that he himself had Jewish ancestry. Since he hated Jews in a disinterested way, he came to hate himself and his family. So he had himself and his family put in concentration camps and killed. This Nazi was consistent. Ima Prescriptivist (in Section 6.4) thought that we couldn't carry the argument further against such a fanatical racist. But we can go further if we criticize the racist's desires.

Step 3 tries to point out flaws (like ignorance or inconsistencies) in Ima's hateful desires. Ima's desires may be based on:

- *current* false beliefs. Ima may think that Aryans are superior and racially pure. We can criticize this on factual grounds.

- *previous* false beliefs. Ima may hate blacks because of previous false beliefs (about blacks or about race). He's given up these beliefs. His hatred of blacks, however, remains.

- social conditioning. Ima may hate blacks because he was taught this as a child. Maybe his family and friends hated blacks, called them names, and promoted false stereotypes about them. And maybe Ima met only a few atypically nasty blacks. Then Ima's hateful desires would diminish if he understood the origin of his hatred and broadened his experience of blacks in an open way.

Ima's anti-black desires remind me of my irrational desire not to eat worms (even when prepared in healthy and appetizing ways). Both desires came from false beliefs or social conditioning. Both would diminish with greater knowledge and experience. Both desires are hard to change. Both are irrational.

We also might have Ima consider other socially taught stereotypes and prejudices. All over the world, people in one group are taught to dislike people in another group. We teach young children:

Be suspicious of *those other people*. They're of a different race (or religion, or ethnic background, or sexual preference, or caste). They aren't our kind. They have strange customs, and do strange things. They're evil and inferior.

When we broaden our knowledge and experience, we conclude, "They're people too, much like us, with many of the same virtues and vices."

The hatreds that are programmed into us from our youth might never disappear; but a wider knowledge and experience will reduce them. That is all that GR needs. Only a very strong hatred of blacks could make Ima desire to be treated as a second-class citizen if he were black. Only with such a hatred could Ima repeat these words and mean them: "I really desire that if I were black then I'd be treated as a second-class citizen." And we can criticize such desires on rational grounds.

So I conclude that Ima won't be a consistent racist if he understands the situation of blacks, vividly and accurately imagines what it would be like to be treated as a second-class citizen in their place, and has his desires rationalized by a wider knowledge and experience. In short: racism is irrational.

But if racism is irrational, why did so many otherwise normal people embrace it? Haas (1988) explained the historical rise of Nazism. Haas talked about the gradual build-up of ancient racial animosities; about nationalism, charismatic leaders, powerful organizations, and social pressures; about fear, greed, hatred, and blind obedience; about lies, stereotypes, ignorance, and uncriticalness; and about how people get used to killing when their friends find it acceptable. Also, the Nazis compartmentalized their thinking. They applied empathy and the golden rule to their own families, but not to Jews. They were rational in choosing means to ends, but not in appraising their ends. This combination of forces was powerful and overcame the weak voice of reason.

The scientist Charles Darwin expressed surprise at how people can be blind to the evil of their racist actions (1839: 35, slightly edited):

> I nearly witnessed an atrocious act that could take place only in a slave country. The slave owner was about to take the women and children from the male slaves, and sell them separately at a public auction at Rio. The inhumanity of separating thirty families never occurred to him. Yet in humanity and good feeling he was superior to most men. There exists no limit to the blindness of selfish habit.

Darwin traced this blindness, in people who professed to be trying to love their neighbor and do God's will, to a lack of empathetic imagination (1839: 526–7, slightly edited):

> Those who look with a cold heart at the slave never put themselves into the position of the latter. Picture your wife and

your little children being torn from you and sold like beasts to the first bidder!

As the scientist Darwin stressed empathetic imagination, so the novelist Harriet Beecher Stowe stressed factual accuracy in this dialogue from *Uncle Tom's Cabin* (1852: 125, slightly edited):

A: "The most dreadful part of slavery is its outrages on the affections – the separating of families, for example."
B: "That's a bad thing," said the other lady. "But it doesn't occur often."
A: "Oh, it does," said the first lady. "I've lived many years in Kentucky and Virginia, and I've seen enough to make one's heart sick. Suppose, ma'am, that your two children be taken from you and sold?"
B: "We can't reason from our feelings to those of this class of persons," said the other lady.

So black slaves don't feel the pain that whites would feel? To rebut this idea, the novel later described how a young slave woman, whose young son was taken from her and sold, was heartbroken and drowned herself.

To guard against racist atrocities, we need knowledge (instead of ignorance and lies), empathetic imagination (instead of insensitivity), and the golden rule (instead of treating others just as a means to our own ends).

9.4 Moral education

Moral education involves teaching moral rules and moral rationality. Ima Intuitionist in Section 4.3 sketched how to teach the former:

> Parents and other adults should teach moral rules to children by their own example, by verbal instruction, by praise and blame, and by reward and punishment.

This is fine, but incomplete, since the same methods can teach bigotry. Our parental example can teach that Jews are to be hated; and we can praise our children when they follow our example and punish them when they act kindly toward Jews. If such training succeeds, our children will end up internalizing Nazi values. It will seem "self-evident" to them that Jews ought to be hated.

Besides teaching *moral rules*, we also need to teach *moral rationality*. The last section claimed that guarding against racist atrocities requires knowledge, imagination, and the golden rule. We can teach these, and other aspects of moral rationality, by personal example and by encouraging certain skills and attitudes. Let me focus on five key commandments of rational moral thinking.

(1) Make informed decisions.

Personal example: Follow this yourself, especially in actions affecting your children. Get to know your children before making decisions about them. This requires communication.

Skills/attitudes: Talk with children about their decisions, and get them to ask questions like: "What are my alternatives?" – "What effect would this have on myself and on others?" – "What are the pros and cons here?" Encourage children to get and reflect on the information needed to make their own decisions.

(2) Live in harmony with your moral beliefs.

Personal example: Take your moral beliefs seriously and put them into practice in your own life. Don't teach your children by your own example to say, "Yes, it's wrong, but I don't care."

Skills/attitudes: Encourage children to take their moral beliefs seriously and follow them conscientiously. Stress the importance of doing the right thing.

(3) Make similar evaluations about similar actions.

Personal example: Apply the same standards to everyone and give reasons for differences in treatment. Respond carefully when you're asked things like, "Mom, why can Jimmy do this but not me?" Don't answer, "Just shut up and do what I say!"

Skills/attitudes: Challenge children to think through their moral dilemmas and to propose principles or reasons (applicable to everyone alike) why actions are right or wrong. Encourage them to apply the same principles to themselves that they apply to others.

(4) Put yourself in the other person's place.

Personal example: Follow this yourself, especially toward your children. Listen sympathetically to them, and try to imagine what their lives are like. This teaches by example how important it is to understand another person's perspective.

Skills/attitudes: Encourage children to listen to others, to share ideas with them, and to reflect on what an action would look like from another person's perspective. Get children to ask questions like, "What would it feel like if I were Suzy and this happened to me?" And have them read stories or watch movies that portray people's lives in a realistic way.

(5) Treat others as you want to be treated.

Personal example: Follow the golden rule yourself, especially toward your children. Reflect on how your actions affect them, imagine yourself in their place, and treat them only as you're willing to be treated by a parent. Don't be seen treating them or others in mean or thoughtless ways – in ways that you don't want to be treated yourself.

Skills/attitudes: Encourage your children to follow the golden rule. Challenge them, when they do something rude or vicious, by asking, "How would you like it if we did that to you?" Help them to think out moral problems in a GR manner.

For those of a religious perspective, these elements would be integrated with religious beliefs and attitudes. And our attempt to grow wiser in our moral thinking would be seen as an attempt to draw closer to God's supreme wisdom.

In these ways, and others that I haven't mentioned, children can be taught to be wiser and more rational in their choices and moral beliefs. This teaching is difficult – but there are many concrete ways to do it. Judging from the low state of moral thinking in the world, it's a task of great importance. Teaching your children to make wise decisions and moral judgments may be one of the most important things that you'll ever do.

9.5 Rationality questions

(Q1) How do we deal with people who say "Yes, I'm inconsistent and irrational; but I don't care about this"?

Some logicians suggest that we hit such people with a stick. A better idea is to pretend to agree: whenever you assert something, also assert the opposite. Soon the irrationalists will want to hit you with a stick.

It's hard to imagine there being sane people who totally reject reason. Such people couldn't drive a car, or keep a job, or cook breakfast – since these all require reason. So people who say "I don't care at all about rationality" probably *do* care.

Many who say they "reject reason" only partly reject it. They may accept reason in part of their life (maybe in their work), but reject it in another part (maybe in their attitudes about other races – where they don't care if they're inconsistent and irrational). In this case, we can at least *try* to reason with them as we did in Section 7.6. We can defend consistency by appealing to things like self-interest, personal feelings, social conventions, God's will, or self-evident truths. They might listen to the self-interest part, especially if we can show that they're likely to lose out in the end by being irrational about their values.

> (Q2) Your approach emphasizes rationality. Do you really think that you've eliminated all the non-rational aspects of our moral thinking?

No, that wasn't my intention. It's clear that there are many cultural and emotional influences on our moral thinking. It isn't so clear how we can reason about moral issues. I'm content to clarify some ways that we can do this – but without denying the cultural and emotional influences.

When people ask how "reason" fits into ethics, they're often asking how *thinking* (as opposed to *feeling*) can contribute. This isn't my question. Instead, I'm asking how we *ought* to make moral judgments. My answer brings in elements like feelings, desires, and imagination.

Reason and morality are weak forces in us; they need powerful allies like feelings, habits, and social approval. We'll have difficulty following the golden rule, for example, unless we develop strong feelings and habits about fairness and concern for others, and have these reinforced by the society around us.

> (Q3) But, ideally, don't you think that morality should depend just on reason?

No. We oversimplify if we make morality depend on just one thing – like feeling, thinking, or religion. Morality ideally involves various "parts" of the self working together – parts such as these:

heart	↔	desires and feelings
eyes	↔	empirical knowledge
right brain	↔	imagination (especially empathy)
ears and mouth	↔	dialogue with others
soul	↔	religious perspective
hands and feet	↔	moral action
left brain	↔	consistency (especially GR)

As we live our moral lives, we have *desires* for ourselves and for others. We have *feelings* about how to live. We have *empirical knowledge* of the world. We *imagine* ourselves in the place of another. We *dialogue* with people who challenge our moral thinking. We sense the higher purpose of morality in *religious* or quasi-religious terms. We try to *act* morally. We look for principles that we can support in a *consistent* way. And we process our thinking and willing for *inconsistencies* of various sorts – and especially for *golden-rule* violations.

Because we tend to be self-centered, GR is especially important. GR has a criticizing function, telling us when our *action* (toward another) conflicts with our *desires* (about how we be treated). GR filters out inconsistencies. For the output of the filter to be of high value, the inputs (knowledge, imagination, desires) have to be of high value; otherwise, we have "junk in and junk out." So consistency is important, and especially GR consistency. But consistency is only one element of rational moral thinking. What we really need is various elements working together.

9.6   Chapter summary

We're *rational* in our moral judgments to the extent that we're consistent, informed, imaginative, and a few more things.

(1) To be consistent includes satisfying things like ends–means consistency, conscientiousness, impartiality, the golden rule, and the formula of universal law.

(2) To be informed is to know the situation (circumstances, alternatives, consequences, and so on); alternative moral views (including arguments for or against them); and ourselves (including how we developed our feelings and moral beliefs).

(3) To be imaginative is to have a vivid and accurate awareness of the situation of another (or of our own situation at a future point of time) and what it would be like to be in that situation. This differs from just knowing facts. It also involves an appreciation of what these facts mean to people's lives.

(4) The "few more things" cover, for example, feeling free to think for ourselves (instead of just conforming); having feelings of concern for ourselves and for others; and dialoging with others.

These rationality conditions (which describe we ought ideally to form our moral beliefs) grow out of our consistency requirements. For example, since we demand that others try to be informed when they deliberate about how to act toward us, we will, if consistent, demand this of ourselves too. So we'll hold the general principle that people ought to be informed when making moral judgments.

These same rationality conditions also apply to desires. Irrational desires have flaws like inconsistency, ignorance, or lack of imagination. Accordingly, racist desires are irrational if they're based on social conditioning and would disappear if we broadened our knowledge and experience.

Our GR attack on racist actions has four steps: (1) Make sure that the racist has a clear understanding of the facts. (2) Have him imagine himself, vividly and accurately, in the place of his victims. (3) If needed, rationalize his desires (about how he'd be treated if he were in their place). (4) See if he treats his victims only as he's willing to be treated in the same situation. The racist will likely fail the GR test.

Helping children to be more rational in their moral thinking is an important part of moral education. It's especially important to teach these five commandments of rational moral thinking: "Make informed decisions," "Live in harmony with your moral beliefs," "Make similar evaluations about similar actions," "Put yourself in the other person's place," and "Treat others as you want to be treated." Adults can teach these by personal example and by promoting the corresponding skills and attitudes in children.

9.7   Study questions

Write out the answers in your ethics folder. If you don't know an answer, go back to the section that deals with it.

1. How can we judge how rational our moral thinking is?
2. Can we ever be fully rational in our moral thinking? (9.1)
3. What does the consistency condition require?
4. What does the information condition require?
5. What does the imagination condition require?
6. Which of the "few more things" strikes you as most important? What might you want to add?
7. What is a "rationality condition?" How can we defend our set of rationality conditions?
8. Give an example where defective desires can block the effectiveness of golden-rule reasoning. How can we criticize such desires? (9.2)
9. Why is the desire not to eat worms held to be irrational? What is the point of this example?
10. Explain the four steps in our GR attack on racism. How can we criticize the desires of a racist who is willing to be treated badly in the place of his victims? (9.3)

11. How does Haas explain why otherwise rational Germans commit-ted racial atrocities against the Jews?
12. How does Darwin explain how ordinary people can be blind to the evil of their racist actions?
13. What three things do we need in order to guard against racist atrocities?
14. How can we teach children to be more rational in their moral judgments? (9.4)
15. How can we deal with someone who professes not to care about being consistent and rational? (9.5)
16. Does the view of moral rationality in the text eliminate all non-rational aspects of our moral thinking?
17. List a few of the dimensions of moral thinking that strike you as particularly important. Are there any further dimensions that you'd like to add?

9.8 For further study

To solidify your understanding, do the computer exercises for "Ethics 09 – Moral Rationality." Also do review exercises "Ethics 09r," "Ethics 09v," and "Ethics 09z." The Computer Exercises appendix at the end of this book has further information on this and on Internet resources.

This chapter is a simplified version of Chapter 7 of Gensler's *Formal Ethics*; see this book for further details and references. Schulman and Mekler's *Bringing Up a Moral Child* has useful suggestions for teaching the golden rule (pages 90–117) and empathetic imagination (pages 52–89); their approach to moral education is in harmony with my approach. Many of the key ideas behind this chapter were inspired by Hare's *Freedom and Reason* and Kant's *Groundwork of the Metaphysics of Morals*. The Bibliography at the end of the book has information on how to find these works.

CHAPTER 10
Consequentialism

CHAPTER 10
Consequentialism

Consequentialism says that we have only one basic duty – namely, to do whatever has the best consequences. In this chapter, we'll first note a few general points about normative ethics and consequentialism. Then we'll consider two important forms of consequentialism: classical utilitarianism and rule utilitarianism. We'll also consider objections to these approaches.

10.1   Normative ethics

So far, we've focused on the nature and methodology of moral judgments (metaethics). We've considered whether morality is based on social conventions, personal feelings, God's will, or self-evident truths. I've argued that, however we view these issues, we should pick out our moral principles in a way that's consistent (which involves the golden rule), informed, imaginative, and so forth. This gives a method for selecting and arguing about moral principles.

Once we have a method, we can use it to arrive at principles about how we ought to live (normative ethics). There are two basic approaches:

- **Consequentialism** says that we ought to do whatever maximizes good consequences. It doesn't in itself matter what kind of thing we do.
- **Nonconsequentialism** says that some kinds of action (such as killing the innocent) are wrong in themselves, and not just wrong because they have bad consequences.

We'll consider consequentialism in this chapter and nonconsequentialism in the next.

Here's an example to illustrate the difference. Suppose that your wife is diagnosed as having terminal cancer; but she doesn't know about this. She asks you about the diagnosis. What should you do? Should you tell her the truth – or should you lie?

If you're a consequentialist, you'll think that you should lie if this has better consequences. So you'd consider whether you wife would be happier knowing or not knowing about her illness. As a consequentialist, you wouldn't think that it's wrong in itself to lie. Instead, you'd think that lying is right if it has better consequences.

If you're a nonconsequentialist, you'll probably think that it's wrong in itself to lie in such cases. Your wife has a right to know, and you'd be treating her wrongly if you lied to her – even if lying would make her happier and thus bring about better consequences.

So should you lie, or shouldn't you? More generally, do consequences alone determine right and wrong? Or are some kinds of action wrong in themselves, and not just wrong because they have bad consequences? This is the most basic issue of normative ethics. How we stand on it will make a big difference to every moral issue that we face (including, for example, issues like abortion or euthanasia).

We'll begin by listening to Ima Utilitarian explain her belief in classical utilitarianism – which is a popular kind of consequentialism.

Classical Utilitarianism:

We ought to do whatever maximizes the balance of pleasure over pain for everyone affected by our action.

10.2   Ima Utilitarian

My name is Ima Utilitarian; but since my boyfriend also has the same first name, I usually go by the name "Util." I've embraced classical utilitarianism as I've come to see that the proper aim of morality is to promote happiness and diminish misery.

I was brought up to believe in strict rules. I was taught, for example, that it was always wrong to steal or lie or break promises or disobey your parents. For a long time I never questioned these things.

Cultural relativism shook up my thinking. The world has many cultures with diverse norms. CR says that we can't objectively evaluate the norms of another culture – since, if we try, then we just evaluate their norms using ours. My first impression was that CR was wrong; we can evaluate norms by their consequences. Suppose that the norms of society A lead to happiness, while those of society B lead to misery. Society A clearly has better norms.

Further study confirmed that happiness was crucial. I learned that enlightened moral thinking is informed, imaginative, and consistent – where consistency involves the golden rule. When we follow GR, we're concerned about the consequences of our actions on others. We try to make others happier, and prevent their misery. So GR leads to utilitarianism. The utilitarian John Stuart Mill (1861: 22) put it this way:

> In the golden rule of Jesus of Nazareth, we read the complete spirit of the ethics of utility. To do as you would be done by, and to love your neighbor as yourself, constitute the ideal perfection of utilitarian morality.

So enlightened moral thinking leads us, first to the golden rule, and then to utilitarianism.

The golden rule isn't the only path to utilitarianism. My boyfriend bases utilitarianism on God's will, since he thinks that God desires our greatest happiness. Others accept the principle as a self-evident truth, or as reflecting their personal feelings.

Precisely stated, **classical utilitarianism** says that we ought always to do whatever maximizes the balance of pleasure over pain for everyone affected by our action. We can apply the principle in two ways – either directly or indirectly.

To apply utilitarianism *directly*, I do three things:

1. I figure out my options. Maybe I could do A or B.
2. I estimate the likely pleasure and pain consequences of each option on the affected parties. Maybe A would make me a little happier but make two others very miserable.
3. I decide which option maximizes the balance of pleasure over pain. This option is my duty.

These steps require a lot of thinking. Step 2 is difficult, since it involves trying to discover the future consequences of our actions. While we can never be sure about these, we can base our judgments on better or worse estimates.

Step 3 can be difficult too, since it involves "adding up" benefits and harms. Some utilitarians talk as if we could put pleasure and pain into numerical units. If this were possible, then we could add up the numbers, using positive ones for pleasure and negative ones for pain, and go with the highest total:

Options ➔	A	B
Tom	+1	-3
Dick	-3	+1
Harry	+4	+5
Total	+2	+3

Utilitarianism
says to do B.

Such calculations would sharpen our moral thinking. But as yet we don't know how to put numbers on pleasure and pain. Instead, we weigh them in our minds, and see intuitively which option maximizes the balance of one over the other. Our opponents say that it's impossible to do this. But we can do it in a rough way; and our opponents have the same problem, since they admit that maximizing good consequences is *one* of our duties (although they recognize other basic duties as well).

It isn't useful to do such direct utilitarian calculations on every action. As I pass each item in the shopping mall, should I do a direct calculation on whether I should steal it? Surely not! It's more useful to apply utilitarianism *indirectly*, by applying a "rule of thumb" about what kinds of action tend to have good or bad results. "Don't steal" is a useful rule of thumb, since stealing tends to have bad results. So, unless circumstances are peculiar, I'll just assume that I ought not to steal.

When should we apply utilitarianism directly? It's useful to do this when we face big decisions. When I chose a college, for example, I listed various schools with their pros and cons; then I picked the place with the biggest balance of pros over cons.

A direct application is also useful when the moral rules conflict. Last week my mother ordered me to reveal what my brother told me in confidence. Here "Obey your parents" and "Don't break confidences" would tell me to do opposite things. So I applied utilitarianism directly. I judged that silence would have better consequences, since it would do less harm to the personal relationships.

It's also useful to apply utilitarianism directly to arrive at moral rules. If we examine particular cases of stealing, we'll find that stealing usually has bad consequences. So "Don't steal" is a useful rule of thumb. So unless we know that a particular act of stealing will maximize good consequences, it's best not to steal.

So yes, I believe in rules; but I don't worship rules. And I don't believe in exceptionless rules. One problem with exceptionless rules is that they sometimes conflict. When I was a child, I was taught "*Always* obey your parents" and "*Never* break confidences"; both were exceptionless. But these prescribed conflicting actions when my mother ordered me to break a confidence. A consistent moral system can't have more than one exceptionless norm; otherwise, it'll lead to contradictions. So the requirement to be consistent in our beliefs eliminates the approach that I was taught as a child.

Another problem is that exceptionless norms can lead to inhumane results in unusual cases. I was taught that stealing is *always* wrong. But suppose that your family will starve unless your father steals a loaf of bread from one who won't miss it. Is stealing then wrong? Do you desire that your father not steal in this case? If you say "yes," then you care more about rules than about human beings. The Pharisees, whom Jesus denounced, insisted on Sabbath rules even when these were harmful to people (see Mark 2:23–7). Do you want to be like the Pharisees?

If you still believe in exceptionless norms, let me give my "Dr Evil" objection. Suppose that, unless you disobey your allegedly exceptionless norm, Dr Evil will torture everyone and then destroy the world. Shouldn't we break your rule in this case? Almost everyone would say "yes." So almost no one could consistently hold exceptionless norms.

Since I think that duty depends on the situation, some accuse me of cultural relativism. But this is confused. I see our duty as depending, not on what our culture tells us, but on what has better consequences. So smoking is wrong if it causes great misery and pain – regardless of whether society approves of it.

10.3   Consequentialisms

This is still Ima (or "Util"). I need to explain why I picked classical (hedonistic) utilitarianism over other forms of consequentialism.

Consequentialism is the general view that we ought to do whatever maximizes good consequences. Consequentialism comes in various flavors. These differ on whether to maximize good results for ourselves only (**egoism**) or for everyone affected by our action (**utilitarianism**) – and on whether to evaluate consequences solely in terms of pleasure and pain (**hedonism**) or in terms of a variety of goods (**pluralism**).

First, whose good should we maximize? Should we do whatever has the best consequences for:

1. ourselves (egoism),
2. our group (family or city or nation or race or …),
3. all humans, or
4. all sentient beings (utilitarianism)?

Since I base my view on the golden rule, and the golden rule applies to our treatment of any sentient being [see Q7 in Section 8.4], I pick option 4 – the utilitarian option.

Consistency gives a solid basis for rejecting egoism. Egoism says "Everyone ought to do whatever maximizes their own self-interest, regardless of how this affects others." To hold this consistently, we'd have to want other people to live that way toward us. So we'd have to desire that X harm us greatly (even paralyze us for life) if this would maximize X's self-interest. But we can't desire this. So we can't consistently accept the principle. So egoism, even though it may remain a temptation, can't be accepted as a rational view about how we ought to live. Similar objections are fatal to options 2 and 3.

Another problem is that egoism is self-defeating. While egoists care much about their own happiness, the egoistic approach is almost guaranteed to make them miserable. If we follow egoism, others will despise us and we'll probably end up despising ourselves. We'll pursue our own happiness better if we strive to promote the good of everyone.

While I reject egoism, I think that there's less conflict between my good and the general good than many people think. Normally I gain happiness when I do good for others, and I suffer when I harm others. And utilitarianism says that I ought to promote my own good when this doesn't clash with the good of another.

A second issue is how to gauge the value of consequences. I accept **hedonism**, which holds that only pleasure is **intrinsically good** (good in itself, abstracting from further consequences) and only pain is intrinsically bad. On hedonism, a thing is good to the extent that:

- it is itself pleasant,
- it produces future pleasure, or
- it prevents future pain.

Painful things, like going to the dentist, can be good if they lead to future pleasure or prevent future pain. Of course, we must consider the long-range consequences of our actions, insofar as we can predict them.

Some people find hedonism shocking. They don't understand that we hedonists use "pleasure" in a wide sense, to include, not just physical pleasures, but any kind of contentment or happiness. Higher pleasures (from friendship, knowledge, and virtue) are more satisfying and enduring than physical pleasures (like eating). It might be less scandalous if we spoke of "promoting happiness"; but the idea would be the same.

Not all utilitarians evaluate consequences by pleasure and pain. Some say that we should maximize:

1. whatever people desire for its own sake (preference view); or
2. many things, like knowledge, virtue, and pleasure (pluralism).

I reject option 1, because people can have bad or foolish desires; some people desire revenge for its own sake. I reject option 2, because I doubt that mere knowledge or virtue in itself, apart from the enjoyment of it, has any intrinsic value. So I accept hedonism.

I should mention moral education. Besides moral rationality [which you read about in the last chapter], we also need to teach moral content. Young children need simple exceptionless rules – for example, that it's always wrong to steal or disobey your parents. Older children need to learn that such rules have exceptions, and that the important thing is to do whatever maximizes happiness and minimizes misery for everyone. So we should teach older children a love for humanity (and other sentient life), rules of thumb for promoting good results, and how to apply utilitarianism directly (by determining options and consequences).

Let me end by listing some advantages of utilitarianism. This view gives a simple and yet flexible way to determine all our duties. It accords with enlightened moral thinking (being informed, imaginative, consistent, and following the golden rule). And it expresses a positive concern for the happiness of all sentient beings.

Before going to Section 10.4, reflect on your initial reaction to utilitarianism. What do you like or dislike about the view? Do you have any objections?

10.4 Bizarre implications

Util (Ima Utilitarian) has given us a clear formulation of an important approach to morality. Her view is simple and intuitive, and it expresses a positive concern for everyone's happiness. But it has bizarre implications that are difficult to accept. So I'll argue that enlightened moral thinking would reject utilitarianism.

Util gave a solid consistency argument against egoism. A similar argument works against utilitarianism. Imagine a town where the lynch mob enjoys hangings so much that it would maximize pleasure if they hanged you for a crime that you didn't commit. Utilitarianism would approve of this act, since it maximizes pleasure. If you were a consistent utilitarian, you'd have to desire that if you were in this situation then you be hanged. Since almost no one can desire this, almost no one can be a consistent utilitarianism. So enlightened moral thinking would reject utilitarianism.

My objection appeals, not to moral intuitions (which utilitarians might not care about), but to consistency. If utilitarians are to hold their view rationally, they must hold it consistently.

Utilitarians could respond to such objections by rejecting their view and moving to another approach – perhaps to one where consequences are important but limited by other duties. Or they could:

(a) bite the bullet (accept the implausible result),
(b) deny that such cases are possible, or
(c) modify utilitarianism.

We'll consider each option.

(a) Utilitarians might say, "I *do* desire that I be hanged in this case to promote the lynch mob's pleasure." But then we can find further objections. Utilitarians will find it difficult to keep biting the bullets.

(b) Utilitarians might say, "Permitting such lynchings would have bad long-range consequences – and so wouldn't really maximize pleasure." But we can suitably adjust the imagined situation to take account of such consequences. Perhaps the politically opportune moment to oppose such lynchings is a year after they lynch you. So it could maximize the total pleasure to lynch you now – and then later to oppose future lynchings. So the example is possible.

Hypothetical cases give the best way to evaluate utilitarianism, since they let us stipulate that a given action maximizes the total pleasure. With *actual* cases, utilitarianism rarely leads to clear results – since long-range consequences are so uncertain.

(c) Utilitarians might say, "I want to modify my view. I now say that sadistic pleasures are intrinsically bad. Thus I can hold that the lynching is *wrong* – since it brings sadistic pleasures to the lynch mob." This modification would get around my lynching example. But other objections may require further modifications.

Our fictional Ima Rule-Utilitarian will take option (c) in the next section. He'll suggest an improved version of utilitarianism that tries to avoid the objections. But before getting there, it will be helpful to sketch some further bizarre implications that utilitarians need to deal with. So here are six more examples.

(1) You're a utilitarian philosopher hired to give a moral justification of slavery. You say, "My job is easy; I just have to make sure that the benefits to the slave owners outweigh the harm to the slaves." So you encourage the slave owners to derive greater enjoyment from having slaves. And you drug the slaves to keep them docile and make them

enjoy being slaves. If slavery maximizes the total pleasure, then utilitarianism approves of it.

(2) You maximize pleasure by killing your miserable rich father and donating his money to buy a park for poor children. Utilitarianism approves of your action.

(3) You're a judge who sentences an innocent man to death for a crime he didn't commit. By discouraging terrorism, your act maximizes the total pleasure. Utilitarianism approves of your action. Utilitarianism permits any harm to the individual for the sake of the general good.

(4) You could bring about the same pleasure and pain results by either honest or dishonest means. Utilitarianism says that it doesn't matter morally which you use.

(5) You hurt someone, because this brings you more pleasure than the pain it causes the other person. Your act has no further pleasure or pain consequences. Utilitarianism says that you acted rightly.

(6) You break a solemn promise because doing so will bring you pleasure. There are no further pleasure or pain consequences. Utilitarianism approves of your act.

Now the fictional Ima Rule-Utilitarian will present his improved form of utilitarianism that tries to avoid such implications.

Pluralistic Rule Utilitarianism:

We should evaluate consequences in terms of various goods, including virtue, knowledge, pleasure, life, and freedom.

We ought to do what would be prescribed by the *rules* with the best consequences for people in society to try to follow.

10.5 Ima Rule-Utilitarian

My name is Ima Rule-Utilitarian. I believe that the goal of morality is to bring about the best consequences for everyone. However, I see "best consequences" in broader terms than just pleasure and pain – and I recognize the usefulness of following strict rules.

You might know my girlfriend, Ima Utilitarian. Since we both have the same first name, I just call her "Util." Now Util has some interesting ideas. She says that morality is about promoting happiness. So we ought always to do whatever maximizes the balance of pleasure over pain for everyone affected by our action. While this sounds good, it has bizarre implications. However, we can avoid these if we make two changes in the view. I suggest that we (a) move from hedonism to pluralism, and (b) move from act to rule utilitarianism.

First, what things are intrinsically good? What things are good in themselves, abstracting from further consequences? It might seem that pleasure is intrinsically good, and pain intrinsically bad. But this has exceptions, since pleasure over the misfortune of another is intrinsically bad. Suppose that your husband is upset over losing his job. It would be intrinsically bad if you felt pleasure over his distress – and intrinsically good if you felt distress over his distress. If so, then we can only say that *normally* pleasure is intrinsically good and pain intrinsically bad.

This brings up the question of methodology: How should we pick out our beliefs about what is intrinsically good? Should we follow our intuitions, or our feelings, or what is socially approved? I suggest rather that we follow a rationality approach. We should try to be as rational as possible (consistent, informed, imaginative, and so forth) and then see what we desire for its own sake. This gives a rational way to pick out our beliefs about intrinsic worth.

This approach leads me to accept **pluralism**, which says that many things are intrinsically good. These include virtue, knowledge, pleasure, life, freedom, and maybe a few more items. Their opposites (vice, ignorance, and so forth) are intrinsically bad.

Util rejects pluralism because she doubts that mere knowledge or virtue in itself, apart from the enjoyment of it, has any intrinsic value. But we often desire knowledge or virtue for its own sake, regardless of whether these include pleasure. And we'd continue to do so if we came to be more rational (consistent, informed, imaginative, and so forth).

Here's an example to show the contrast between hedonism and pluralism. Imagine two lives equal in pleasure. In the first life, your pleasure is mindless and comes from a "pleasure machine" that stimulates your brain. In the second life, you have the same amount of pleasure, but it comes from a normal exercise of your higher powers. Almost everyone would prefer the second life, even though both have the same amount of pleasure. So our preferences are pluralistic – not hedonistic. And it's hard to imagine that these preferences would change if we became more rational. So it seems that our rational preferences would support the pluralistic view.

My argument concedes to hedonism that we can make sense of the phrase "two lives *equal* in pleasure." In practice, though, "amount of pleasure" is very vague. To see this, ask yourself how much pleasure you're experiencing right now. And adding up "pleasure units" is a very doubtful enterprise.

Let me digress about another error of hedonism – its identification of happiness with pleasure. This idea is entirely wrong; being happy is *not* the same as having pleasure. We might have lots of pleasures but be quite unhappy – since we see our life of pleasure as ultimately meaningless. Or we might have few pleasures but be happy – since we see our life as meaningful in some deeper way.

I'd define happiness as an overall contentment with our life. So it's a kind of contentment, but deeper than pleasure. Pleasure doesn't necessarily bring happiness. Neither does money, at least according to many who have it; the rich are almost as often dissatisfied with their lives as are the poor. As I see it, the key to being happy is to live right; contentment is a byproduct of right living. Our personal contentment shouldn't be our major focus. If we focus too much on our own contentment, then we'll probably end up miserable. Instead, we should try to live properly – be concerned for others, do meaningful things, and so forth – and this will probably bring contentment. I'd go further and say that the key to being happy is to live in the pluralistic rule-utilitarian way. But I have to explain what this is.

Let's first see how the pluralistic approach to value helps us to avoid bizarre implications. On classical utilitarianism, these three actions would be right if they maximized the total balance of pleasure over pain:

0. A lynch mob hangs you for a crime that you didn't commit – because it gets great pleasure from this.
1. You keep slaves (whom you drug so that they enjoy being slaves) – since this brings your family great pleasure.
2. You kill your miserable rich father and donate his money to buy a park for poor children.

On our approach, all three actions would be wrong. In case 0, the lynch mob's sadistic pleasures are intrinsically bad and your life (which is taken away) is intrinsically good; so the lynching has very bad consequences. In case 1, freedom is intrinsically good; so you harm the slaves greatly if you take away their freedom (even though you give them pleasure). In case 2, the life of your father is intrinsically good; so you harm him if you take his life.

So we can avoid many problems by switching from hedonism to pluralism. But there are still a few problems – like this example:

2a.   You kill your miserable rich father and donate part of his
      money to buy a park for poor children and part of his money
      to fund medical research for some rare disease (which saves
      some lives in the long run). Since your action both maximizes
      pleasure and saves lives, it maximizes good consequences.

I can't accept that this killing would be right. Fortunately, the "rule
utilitarian" part of my view gets me out of the problem.
    Let me distinguish between the normal kind of utilitarianism (called
"act utilitarianism") and my approach ("rule utilitarianism"):

- **Act utilitarianism (AU)** says that we ought to do the *act* with
  the best consequences.
- **Rule utilitarianism (RU)** says that we ought to do what
  would be prescribed by the *rules* with the best consequences
  for people in society to try to follow.

RU takes a two-step approach to determining our duty. First, we ask
what rules would have the best consequences for people in society to try
to follow. As we answer this, we should keep in mind the imperfections
and limitations of human beings. Second, we apply these rules to our
action. I'll argue that RU's two-step approach avoids AU's bizarre
implications and has better consequences for society.
    Classical utilitarians have little respect for rules. They scorn excep-
tionless norms. They see moral rules only as loose "rules of thumb"
about what kinds of action tend to have good or bad results. They're
prepared to break any rule when doing so seems to have better results.
    We rule utilitarians, in contrast, have little respect for speculation
about what maximizes good consequences. People too easily talk themselves into doing foolish things for the sake of good results. It would
have much better results in the long run if people followed strict or even
exceptionless rules.
    What rule would be most useful for society to follow about killing?
Let me give you the act utilitarian and rule utilitarian options:

AU Killing is right if and only if it has the best consequences.
RU Killing is strictly wrong, with perhaps exceptions for a few
    carefully defined cases (like self-defense).

A rule against killing needs to be firm and definite; otherwise, people
will twist it for their own purposes. I'd be afraid to live in a society that
followed the AU rule – where people would kill whenever they speculated that this would have better results. People would apply this in

irresponsible ways, with disastrous effects. It would have better results in the long run if society followed a strict rule against killing.

Let's get back to case 2a:

2a. You kill your miserable rich father and donate part of his money to buy a park for poor children and part of his money to fund medical research for some rare disease (which saves some lives in the long run). Since your action both maximizes pleasure and saves lives, it maximizes good consequences.

We rule utilitarians *condemn* the killing. The rule behind this action (that you can kill if you think it has better consequences) would bring social disaster and ruin. As I noted in the previous paragraph, it would have better results if society followed a strict rule against killing.

Consider the example of the judge:

4. You're a judge who sentences an innocent man to death for a crime he didn't commit. By discouraging terrorism, your act maximizes the total pleasure. Classical utilitarianism approves of your action.

Again, we rule utilitarians *condemn* this action. In real life, judges don't know whether sentencing the innocent will have the best consequences. They can only guess, or speculate. Such speculation generally backfires and has very bad consequences. It would have better results in the long run if judges, instead of speculating about future consequences, simply followed a rule *never* to sentence an innocent person to death.

So we rule utilitarians think that in many areas it has better results to apply strict or even exceptionless rules. Let me give two more examples. First consider rules about drugs. It would have better results if people followed the second rule instead of the first:

AU Take heroin for recreational purposes if and only if this has the best consequences.
RU Never take heroin for recreational purposes.

People who are tempted to take drugs tend to be poor decision-makers. If they calculate consequences, instead of following a hard and fast rule, they'll more easily yield to temptation. They'll give in to peer pressure when their friends talk about the good consequences of drugs. So they'll become drug addicts and ruin their lives. It has better results to follow the second rule: "Just say no."

152 ETHICS

Or suppose that you're a happily married man who dearly loves his family. You're away on a trip and are tempted to infidelity. It would have better results if you followed the second rule instead of the first:

AU Commit adultery if and only if this has the best consequences.
RU Don't commit adultery.

Men who are tempted to infidelity are notoriously bad decision-makers. They too easily convince themselves that infidelity will have the best consequences. They too easily say to themselves, "A one-night stand will be pleasant and have no future bad results." But this act, of course, is apt to have *very* bad results; it's apt to destroy your marriage, and hurt you and the people you love. Again, it would have better results to follow the second rule: "Just say no."

Let me sum up. My improved version of utilitarianism claims that:

- We should evaluate consequences in terms of various goods, including virtue, knowledge, pleasure, life, and freedom.
- We ought to follow the *rules* with the best consequences for society to follow.

My version of utilitarianism is better because (a) it avoids the bizarre implications of classical utilitarianism and (b) its stress on strict rules would in the long run have better results for society.

Before going to Section 10.6, reflect on your initial reaction to rule utilitarianism. What do you like or dislike about the view? Do you have any objections?

10.6 RU problems

Is pluralistic rule utilitarianism an acceptable approach? It surely seems better than classical utilitarianism. Its pluralistic approach to intrinsic value makes sense. And it has a deeper understanding of human psychology. It sees that humans, without strict rules, will often talk themselves into doing foolish things.

RU *seems* to avoid the bizarre implications. It's difficult to be sure about this, because it's difficult to know what RU would lead to. Applying the "maximize good consequences" test to rules isn't much easier than applying it to individual actions. In many cases, we can only guess at the long-range results of following one rule instead of another.

I have two objections to rule utilitarianism. First, suppose that people in your society were very stupid, and it was useful to teach them only very simplistic moral rules. Why should you, who are more intelligent, have a duty to follow these simplistic rules – especially if you could produce better results by breaking them? I'm not sure how a rule utilitarian would answer this question.

Second, rule utilitarianism, even if it would generally lead to the right judgments, would seem to do so for the wrong reasons. *Why* is it wrong to kill your father in case 2a (where you donate his money to fund a park and medical research)? Is this action wrong just because it's socially useful to have a strict rule against killing? What if this were not so? What if the rules that were most socially useful would permit killing your father? Then would killing your father be right? It's hard to believe that it would be. The belief that this would be right would seem to violate GR consistency.

Nonconsequentialists have a simple answer to why it's wrong to kill your father in case 2a. They say that it's wrong in itself to kill an innocent human being. This wrongness doesn't depend on any lucky fact about the social usefulness of a strict rule against killing.

Ima Rule-Utilitarian suggested the following methodology for justifying his pluralistic approach to intrinsic value:

> We should try to be as rational as possible (consistent, informed, imaginative, and so forth) and then see what we desire for its own sake. This gives a rational way to pick out our beliefs about intrinsic worth.

When we follow this, we seem to desire, abstracting from further consequences, that certain kinds of action (such as killing the innocent or breaking promises) not be done. So Ima's suggestion would lead us to believe that these kinds of action are bad in themselves (and not just bad because the rule against them happens to be socially useful). So Ima's suggestion would seem to lead to nonconsequentialism.

If we reject rule utilitarianism, as I think we should, we may want to incorporate some of its ideas into a better approach to normative ethics.

10.7 Chapter summary

Consequentialism says that we ought to do whatever maximizes good consequences. It doesn't in itself matter what kind of thing we do. What matters is that we maximize good results.

One popular kind of consequentialism is classical (hedonistic) utilitarianism. This view says that we ought always to do whatever maximizes the balance of pleasure over pain for everyone affected by our action. This view could be based on the golden rule, which leads us to be concerned about the happiness and misery of others. Or it could be based on God's will, self-evident truths, or our own personal feelings.

We can apply utilitarianism directly (by first estimating the likely consequences of each option and then picking the option with the best consequences) or indirectly (by applying a "rule of thumb" about what kinds of action tend to have good or bad results). Many utilitarians reject exceptionless rules. They think that any rule should be broken when it has better consequences to do so. So they see moral rules only as loose "rules of thumb."

Despite its plausibility, utilitarianism has many bizarre implications; these make it difficult to hold the view in a consistent way. For example, imagine a town where the lynch mob enjoys hangings so much that it maximizes pleasure to hang you for a crime that you didn't commit. Would it then be right to hang you? Utilitarians can respond to such objections by biting the bullet (accepting the implausible result), denying that such cases are possible, or modifying utilitarianism.

Pluralistic rule utilitarianism is a modified form of utilitarianism. It rejects hedonism (that only pleasure is intrinsically good). Instead, it accepts a pluralistic view of value (that many things are intrinsically good, including virtue, knowledge, pleasure, life, and freedom). This view also says that we ought to do what would be prescribed by the *rules* with the best consequences for people in society to try to follow. It says that we'll live better if we follow strict rules in areas like killing or drugs. Without strict rules, we'll too often talk ourselves into doing foolish things. Rule utilitarians claim that their approach avoids the bizarre implications and produces better consequences.

It may be objected that rule utilitarianism, even if it would lead to the right judgments, would do so for the wrong reasons. RU opposes killing the innocent – on the grounds that socially useful rules would forbid such actions. But what if socially useful rules permitted such actions? Then would killing the innocent be right? The belief that this would be right would seem to violate GR consistency. So wouldn't it be better to hold that killing the innocent is *wrong in itself*?

10.8 Study questions

Write out the answers in your ethics folder. If you don't know an answer, go back to the section that deals with it.

1. Explain the difference between consequentialism and nonconsequentialism. (10.1)
2. What is (classical) utilitarianism? (10.2)
3. How did the study of cultural relativism first lead Ima Utilitarian toward utilitarianism?
4. How did the golden rule confirm Ima's belief in utilitarianism? What other paths could bring one to utilitarianism?
5. Explain the direct and indirect ways to apply utilitarianism. When should we use the direct method?
6. Why did Ima reject exceptionless norms?
7. How do egoistic and utilitarian forms of consequentialism differ? Why did Ima reject egoism? (10.3)
8. What was Ima's view about what is intrinsically good? What is pluralism and why did she reject it?
9. Write about a page sketching your initial reaction to utilitarianism. Does it seem plausible to you? What do you like and dislike about it? Can you think of any way to show that it's false?
10. Explain the "lynching is fun" objection to utilitarianism. How does it involve consistency? (10.4)
11. In what ways could a utilitarian respond to such objections?
12. Among the other objections to utilitarianism, which two do you take to be the strongest?
13. What does pluralism hold? Why might one prefer this view to hedonism? (10.5)
14. What are some objections to equating happiness with pleasure? What definition of happiness is given in the text?
15. Give an example of how pluralism helps us to avoid objections to classical utilitarianism.
16. What is rule utilitarianism? Explain how it applies to the "killing your father" example.
17. Why does rule utilitarianism advocate that we follow strict or even exceptionless principles? Give an example of such a rule.
18. Write about a page sketching your initial reaction to pluralistic rule utilitarianism. Does it seem plausible to you? What do you like and dislike about it? Can you think of any way to show that it's false?
19. Explain the two objections to rule utilitarianism. (10.6)

10.9   For further study

To solidify your understanding, do the computer exercises for "Ethics 10 – Consequentialism." The Computer Exercises appendix at the end of this book has further information on this and on Internet resources.

Mill's brief book *Utilitarianism* is the classic statement of the view; Smart's brief "Utilitarianism" is a more recent defense. Brandt's short "In search of a credible form of utilitarianism" is a good statement of one form of rule utilitarianism; Hare's longer *Moral Thinking* attempts to bridge act and rule utilitarianism. Be forewarned that there are many forms of rule utilitarianism. Aristotle's *Nichomachaen Ethics* (especially Book 1) is the classic treatment of happiness; Brandt's short "Happiness" is a more recent account. The Bibliography at the end of the book has information on how to find these works.

CHAPTER 11
Nonconsequentialism

CHAPTER 11
Nonconsequentialism

Ross's Prima Facie View:

The basic moral principles say that we ought, other things being equal, to do or not to do certain kinds of things: keep our promises, do good to others, not harm others, and so forth.

Nonconsequentialism says that some kinds of action (such as killing the innocent or breaking promises) are wrong in themselves, and not just wrong because they have bad consequences. Such things may be exceptionlessly wrong, or may just have some independent moral weight against them. Some nonconsequentialists (like the eighteenth-century German philosopher Immanuel Kant) support exceptionless rules. Others (like the twentieth-century British philosopher W.D. Ross) support only weaker prima facie rules.

We'll begin by listening to the fictional Ima Rossian defend Ross's approach. Then we'll consider some objections – especially ones that might be made from the "exceptionless rules" perspective. Finally, we'll look into some further areas of normative ethics, including distributive justice, virtues, and rights.

11.1 Ima Rossian

My name is Ima Rossian. I've been trying to trying to steer between the "exceptionless duties" approach to morality that I was taught as a child and the utilitarianism of my roommate; both of these lead to absurd results. I've found a more sensible approach in the "prima facie view" of the British philosopher W.D. Ross.

A **prima facie duty** is a duty that holds if other things are equal. More precisely, it's a factor that tends in itself to make something our duty but can sometimes be overridden by other factors. Ross's **prima facie view** says that the basic moral principles are about prima facie duties. Other things being equal, we ought to keep our promises, do good to others, not harm others, and so forth. On this approach, what matters in ethics is, not just consequences, but also what kind of thing we do.

Ross says that breaking promises is wrong in itself. Violating our word is wrong, not just because it tends to have bad consequences, but because of the kind of act that it is. So keeping promises is an independent duty, not just a "rule of thumb" to promote good consequences. But it isn't our only duty, and other duties can conflict with it. In order to fulfill other duties that are more urgent, we sometimes ought to break a promise.

Here's an example. I promised my boyfriend to go hiking with him on the Brecksville trails after school; we both looked forward to seeing the beautiful fall colors. Since I promised, I felt some obligation or duty to do as I promised. But how strong was the obligation? What would it take to justify violating it?

The "exceptionless duties" view says that I ought to keep my promises no matter what. This is crazy. Suppose that I get home after school and find that my mother is sick and needs to be taken to the hospital – and I'm the only one who can take her. Should I say, "Sorry Mom, but I can't take you; you'll just have to suffer and die – because I promised to go hiking and the duty to keep promises holds without exception"? No way! My duty to help my mother is stronger than my duty to keep the promise. Unless my boyfriend is an absolute jerk, he'll understand this.

So I reject exceptionless duties. I agree with my roommate Ima Utilitarian about this. There can't be exceptionless duties, she argues, because such duties:

1. would conflict and thus lead to contradictions,
2. would lead to inhumane results in unusual cases, and
3. should be violated if we need to do this to keep Dr Evil from torturing everyone and then destroying the world.

This seems conclusive to me. But I differ with her on further points.

Ima Utilitarian explains exceptions in terms of consequences. She sees moral norms as "rules of thumb" about how to promote good results. While such rules can be helpful, we should break them whenever doing so has better consequences. In the case about driving my mother to the hospital, it clearly has better consequences to break the rule about keeping promises.

This sounds sensible, until you think about it more carefully. Utilitarians say that it's all right to break a serious promise whenever doing so has *slightly* better consequences. This doesn't take seriously enough the duty to keep promises. When we promise something, we take on a special obligation to another person. We may have to break a promise in some cases; but a slight gain in good consequences won't justify breaking it. Keeping our word is a serious duty.

Suppose that I baby-sit for your child, so that you and your wife can go to a concert. You promise to pay me a certain amount of money. But you discover that you could bring about slightly better consequences by giving the money to the poor instead of to me – since the benefit to the poor would outweigh my disappointment. Utilitarianism says that you should give the money to the poor, since this maximizes good consequences. The fact that you promised carries no special moral weight. But this is absurd. If you promise to pay me, then that creates a strong obligation. I'd protest if people took so lightly the promises that they make to me.

So for promise-keeping at least, Ross's prima facie view is more sensible than either the "exceptionless norms" view or utilitarianism.

11.2 Our basic duties

This is still Ima Rossian. I need another section to tell you about Ross's basic duties.

Some of his duties are about doing good or harm. To fill this out, we need to talk about what is intrinsically good. Ross was a pluralist and accepted three main intrinsic goods: virtue, knowledge, and pleasure. I'd like to add life and freedom. So to do good to another is to promote the virtue, knowledge, pleasure, life, or freedom of the other person. And to do harm is to bring vice, ignorance, pain, death, or bondage.

Ross recognized seven basic prima facie duties:

1. **Fidelity**: Keep your promises.
2. **Reparation**: Make up for any harm you've done to another.
3. **Gratitude**: Return good to those who have done good to you.
4. **Justice**: Upset distributions of pleasure or happiness that don't accord with merit.
5. **Beneficence**: Do good to others.
6. **Self-improvement**: Improve your virtue and knowledge.
7. **Nonmaleficence**: Don't harm others.

Other things being equal, we ought to follow these norms. When just one norm applies, that one gives our duty. But sometimes the norms conflict. In the example about my mother, fidelity and benevolence prescribed conflicting things:

- Fidelity would say to keep my promise to go hiking (which involves not driving my mother to the hospital).
- Beneficence would say to drive my mother to the hospital (which involves breaking my promise to go hiking).

When our duties conflict, we have to follow the stronger duty. Here the strong benefit to my mother outweighs the casual promise. So I broke the promise.

Ross's principles make sense to me, with two exceptions. First, I just don't get his justice principle. If my brothers and sisters aren't happy in proportion to their virtue (the most virtuous being happiest, the second most virtuous being second happiest, and so forth), should I try to upset this? Does Ross really mean this? I think we need a better justice rule.

Ross is unsure whether to include promoting our own enjoyment under the self-improvement duty; he says that we promote our own enjoyment enough already. Ross has obviously never met my mother – who really ought to go out and enjoy herself sometimes; maybe then she wouldn't get so sick. I'd include a duty to promote our own enjoyment, and base it on the self-regard principle [see Q8 of Section 8.4].

Other duties flow from these basic ones. When we talk, we make an implicit promise not to tell lies; and so we have a duty not to tell lies. And we make an implicit promise to obey the laws of the country where we live; and so we have a duty to obey the law. This latter duty also derives in part from gratitude (for benefits received from the country) and beneficence (to cooperate in promoting the general good).

Ross is an intuitionist; he bases his duties on moral intuitions. When the duties conflict, we appeal to intuitions to find out which duty is stronger. This is the weakest part of Ross's view, and the part most often criticized. People's moral intuitions vary greatly, and the view gives no way to criticize defective intuitions (for example, racist intuitions).

We get a stronger view if we replace Ross's intuitionism with a method that appeals to rationality (being consistent, informed, imaginative, and so forth [as in Chapters 7 to 9]). Rationality would endorse most of Ross's duties. Since we demand that others practice fidelity, reparation, gratitude, and so forth toward us, we will, if consistent, demand these things of ourselves too – and we'll regard them as duties.

Rationality can give useful guidance when the norms conflict. In the case about my mother, golden-rule consistency would practically force me to think that I ought to break the promise and drive my mother to the hospital.

Ross sees some basic duties as stronger than others. Nonmaleficence is normally stronger than beneficence. In general, it's not right to harm one person to help another or to promote social usefulness. One of the defects of utilitarianism is that it permits any harm to the individual for the sake of maximizing pleasure. Ross's view fixes this defect.

Often our duties are relational, in the sense that they depend on how we're related to the other person. We have special duties to X if we made a promise to X, or hurt X, or if X helped us, or if X is our spouse or child or friend. Each relationship leads to special duties. Utilitarianism wrongly sees such personal relationships as morally irrelevant; our only duty is to maximize good consequences. So utilitarianism doesn't do justice to the personal and relational aspects of duty.

The main drawback to Ross's approach is that it doesn't give us clear answers to most moral questions. But the other views aren't any better on this. The "exceptionless duties" view gives us clear answers, but it leads to contradictions when its norms conflict. Utilitarianism would give us clear answers if we knew the long-range consequences of our actions; but this is beyond human knowledge.

Consider how Ross's view applies to killing. By nonmaleficence, it's wrong to bring something intrinsically bad to another. Since death is intrinsically bad, it's wrong to bring death to another. So killing is wrong. But how wrong? Can our duty to protect our own life outweigh the duty not to kill another? Can it be right to kill in self-defense? What about capital punishment, abortion, and mercy killing? Ross's view is vague on such issues. While his view gives a general framework for seeing our duties, we still need to work out (in a consistent, informed, and imaginative way) specific duties on areas like killing.

In spite of this vagueness, Ross's view has many strengths. It gives a balanced perspective that accords closely with what most intelligent, reflective people believe about our duties.

Before going to Section 11.3, reflect on your initial reaction to Ross's prima facie view. What do you like or dislike about it? Do you have any objections?

11.3 Exceptionless norms

Ima has given us a clear formulation of an important approach to morality. I agree with much of what she says, including her criticisms. She says that Ross's view needs a better justice rule (we'll work on this later) and that the view is vague when applied to specific moral issues.

Another problem with Ross's view, in my opinion, is its rejection of strict or exceptionless rules – a feature it borrowed from classical utilitarianism. Ross didn't mention *rule* utilitarianism, which in his time hadn't been developed very far. I favor combining Ross's view with some rule utilitarian ideas about the importance of strict rules.

Ima Rossian and her roommate had three arguments against exceptionless duties. There can't be exceptionless duties, they argued, because such duties:

1. would conflict and thus lead to contradictions,
2. would lead to inhumane results in unusual cases, and
3. should be violated if we need to do this to keep Dr Evil from torturing everyone and then destroying the world.

But these arguments fall apart if we examine them carefully.

(1) "There can't be exceptionless duties, because they'd conflict and thus lead to contradictions." The norms that Ima was taught as a child did indeed conflict; but not all groups of exceptionless norms conflict. Consider these three norms from Ima Rule-Utilitarian:

- Never kill an innocent person.
- Never take heroin for recreational purposes.
- Never commit adultery.

These won't conflict. So it's consistent to accept a few exceptionless norms, so long as they're formulated carefully.

(2) "There can't be exceptionless duties, because these would lead to inhumane results in unusual cases." Ima pointed out how "Stealing is *always* wrong" would forbid you to steal a loaf of bread to keep your family from starving. Surely it would be all right to steal in this case.

I agree that we should avoid exceptionless norms that have inhumane results. I propose consistency as the test of "inhumane results": can we desire that the norm be followed even if we imagine ourselves (or our family) in such and such a place in the situation? If we can't desire this, then we're inconsistent in holding the norm. Ima's example shows that it would be difficult to hold "Stealing is *always* wrong" consistently.

The most plausible exceptionless norms are ones that *forbid* seriously inhumane actions. Recall that both Socrates and Jesus were innocent and yet, for utilitarian reasons, were put to death. "Never kill an innocent person" is designed to stop such inhumane actions.

Would "Never kill an innocent person" itself sometimes have inhumane results? Some think so, and bring up examples like mercy killing. If I were convinced by these examples (which I am not), then I'd support an anti-killing rule with more qualifications – perhaps one like (b) instead of (a):

(a) Never kill an innocent person.
(b) Never kill someone except in self-defense or mercy killing.

I regard both norms as "exceptionless" (even though they have built-in restrictions) because they're formulated using "never."

So if a proposed exceptionless norm is found to have inhumane results in unusual cases, we can revise the norm to avoid the results – and then claim that the revised norm holds in all cases. Of course, it may be difficult to think of all the needed qualifications; but this doesn't show that exceptionless norms are impossible.

(3) "There can't be exceptionless duties, because any rule – even one against killing the innocent – should be violated if we need to do this to keep Dr Evil from torturing everyone and then destroying the world." We could answer this objection in one of three ways:

- We could bite the bullet – and insist that we shouldn't kill the innocent even to stop Dr. Evil from destroying the world.

- We could qualify the norm to avoid the objection. To do this, we could either add a disaster clause (as in "Never kill the innocent unless this is needed to prevent disaster") or else insist that our norm is intended to cover only actual cases (and not fantastic Dr Evil ones).

- We could insist that, even if there are highly unusual cases where killing the innocent is justifiable, still in real life we don't know enough to be able to recognize these cases. So we'll make better decisions if we follow the practical rule *never* to kill the innocent; following this rule strictly will prevent many tragic mistakes. (This answer is in the spirit of rule utilitarianism.)

For practical purposes, it doesn't matter which answer we give. In all three cases, we'll make the same decisions on practical cases.

When should we take a norm as very strict, or even as exceptionless? I suggest this principle:

> Take a norm more strictly if doing so would tend to prevent great evils or foolish choices.

Here "great evils" would cover things like the killing of an innocent person, the bringing about of a drug addiction, or the ruining of a happy marriage. When such things are at stake, and when following a looser rule is apt to lead to bad choices (see Section 10.5), it makes sense to follow a strict or even exceptionless rule.

It's important to insist that some moral rules should be taken very strictly. Many of the problems in the world today come from the fact that a lot of people take moral rules very loosely – and thus can talk themselves into doing almost anything.

11.4   Distributive justice

How ought goods to be distributed in a society? We noticed problems with Ross's view on distributive justice. So we'll here consider three further views – first utilitarianism, and then the nonconsequentialist views of John Rawls and Robert Nozick.

Classical utilitarianism says that we ought to maximize the balance of pleasure over pain. If our action maximizes good, it doesn't matter how equal or unequal the distribution of good is. So utilitarianism could in principle justify a wide gap between rich and poor. WB, IMF, WTO

Utilitarians, however, claim that their view in practice prefers a more equal distribution. Consider a simple island society with two families. The rich family earns $999,000 a year and has abundant goods; the poor family earns $1000 a year and is close to starvation. Suppose that $1000 from the rich family went to the poor family. The poor family would benefit greatly, and the rich family would hardly notice the loss. The reason for this is the **diminishing marginal utility** of money; as we get richer, each extra dollar makes less difference to how well we live. Going from $999,000 to $998,000 matters little, while going from $1000 to $2000 makes a big difference. Thus, utilitarians argue, a given amount of wealth tends to produce more total happiness if it's spread out more evenly. Our island society would probably maximize its total happiness if both families shared their wealth equally.

While this seems sensible, nonconsequentialists are suspicious. If one family gets more pleasure out of a given amount of money than another, should it then get more money (since this would maximize the total enjoyment)? Is this fair? And even if utilitarianism leads to the right judgments on equality, does it do so for the right reasons? Is equality good, not in itself, but merely because it produces the biggest total?

John Rawls has proposed an influential *nonconsequentialist* approach to justice. How can we decide what is just? Rawls suggests that we ask what rules we'd agree to under certain hypothetical conditions (the **original position**). Imagine that we're free, clearheaded, and know all the relevant facts – but don't know our own place in society (whether rich or poor, black or white, male or female). The knowledge limitation is meant to insure impartiality. If we don't know our race, for example, we can't manipulate the rules to favor our race over others. The rules of justice are the rules that we'd agree to under these impartial conditions.

What rules would we agree to in the original position? Rawls argues that we'd pick these two basic principles of justice (which I've simplified in their wording):

- **Equal liberty principle:** Society ought to safeguard the greatest liberty for each person compatible with an equal liberty for all others.

- **Difference principle:** Society ought to promote the equal distribution of wealth, except for inequalities that serve as incentives to benefit everyone (including the least advantaged group) and are open to everyone on an equal basis.

The equal liberty principle insures things like freedom of religion and freedom of speech. Such rights, Rawls says, are not to be violated for the sake of social usefulness. The difference principle is about how to distribute wealth. From the original position, we might be attracted to the egalitarian view, that everyone should have the exact same wealth. But society would stagnate that way, since people would have little incentive to do difficult things (like become doctors or inventors) that ultimately benefit everyone. So we'd prefer a rule that permits incentives.

In a Rawlsian society, everyone would have roughly the same wealth – except for equalities (like more pay for doctors) that are justified as incentives that ultimately benefit everyone, and that are open to everyone on an equal basis.

Robert Nozick is the sharpest critic of Rawls's difference principle. He proposes the **entitlement view** of just possessions. This says that whatever you earn fairly, through hard work and just agreements, is yours. If everyone has legitimately earned what they have, then the resulting distribution is just – regardless of how unequal it may be. No one has a right to take your possessions away from you, even if others have far less. Schemes (like a progressive income tax) that force a redistribution of wealth are wrong, because they violate your right to property. They steal from you in order to give to others.

How much should doctors get paid? On Nozick's approach, they should get paid whatever they legitimately earn. In one society, they may earn about the same as everyone else; in another, they may earn huge amounts of money. In both cases, they're entitled to what they earn – and any scheme to take away their earnings to help others is unjust.

Which view should we prefer, Rawls's or Nozick's? If we appealed to moral intuitions, we'd have a deadlock; liberal intuitions accord with Rawls, while libertarian intuitions accord with Nozick. I'd claim, however, that rational consistency would favor something like Rawls's view. Imagine a society organized on Nozick's free-market approach, in which, after several generations, there's a huge gap between rich and poor. Those born into a rich family are rich, and those born into a poor family suffer from a poverty that they can't overcome. Imagine yourself and your family suffering from this poverty. Can you desire that, if you were in this condition, then the Nozickian principles be followed?

11.5   Ten commandments

It may be helpful to compare the norms that we've collected with the world's most influential list of duties: the ten commandments.

Our philosophical norms divide into two groups. The first group (from Chapters 7 to 9) gives a method for reasoning about and picking out other moral judgments:

> Be consistent (in a broad sense that involves being conscientious and impartial and following the golden rule), informed, imaginative, and so forth.

Using this as a basis, we defended a rough and incomplete list of further goods, duties, and rights:

- Intrinsic goods: virtue, knowledge, pleasure, life, and freedom – and maybe a few more things that we missed.
- Ross's prima facie duties: fidelity, reparation, gratitude, beneficence, self-improvement, and nonmaleficence.
- The principle that we should take a norm more strictly if doing so would tend to prevent great evils or foolish choices.
- Justice duties: the equal liberty and difference principles.

To these, I'd like to add two further norms. Act and rule utilitarianism can be good ways to think through a moral issue, as long as we see that they can be outweighed by other duties. So I suggest adding these as prima facie duties:

AU   If you can trust your judgment about what individual act has
     the best consequences, then do this act – unless this violates a
     stronger duty.

RU   If you can't trust your judgment about what individual act has
     the best consequences, then follow the rule with the best con-
     sequences to apply in such cases – unless this violates a
     stronger duty.

AU would apply more to decisions that we can carefully research, while
RU would apply more to training our moral habits.

Nonconsequentialism is messy. It lacks the simplicity of classical
utilitarianism, with its single norm: "Maximize the balance of pleasure
over pain." But the truth isn't always simple.

The ten commandments divide into duties to God and duties to
human beings. Subdividing the latter, we get this:

Duties to God	1. Thou shalt not worship false gods.
	2. Thou shalt not take God's name in vain.
	3. Keep holy the Sabbath.
Duties to family	6. Thou shalt not commit adultery.
	4. Honor thy father and thy mother.
Duties to anyone	5. Thou shalt not kill.
	7. Thou shalt not steal.
	8. Thou shalt not bear false witness.
Duties to yourself	9. Thou shalt not covet thy neighbor's wife.
	10. Thou shalt not covet thy neighbor's goods.

The Bible recognizes many further duties beyond these ten (for example,
gratitude and reparation). But these ten are seen as especially important.

The philosophical and Biblical lists have different goals. The philosophical list tries to give a comprehensive but general account of all our
duties. The Biblical list, in contrast, tries to give the most important of
our specific duties. While the two lists have no items in common, they
fit together nicely and offer mutually enriching insights. Both lists can
be based on the golden rule.

The first group of commandments gives duties toward God. Other
such duties include faith, hope, and love; obedience; and prayerful
responses of praise and thanksgiving. Our duties to other people are
indirectly duties to God, since they express obedience to him and concern
for his creatures.

While our philosophical list doesn't mention duties to God, it could, presuming a belief in God, lead to such duties. For example, we'd have duties of gratitude to respond to God's goodness – and duties of rationality to follow the will of a supremely wise being. St. Augustine claimed that the golden rule would lead us to love God; we surely desire that if we were in God's place then we would be loved by our creatures.

The second group gives duties to one's family, seen in traditional terms as a husband, wife, and children. For a family to flourish, the bond between husband and wife must be strong. So adultery is forbidden; few things can destroy a family more quickly. Further duties include affection, communication, and time together – and avoiding physical and mental cruelty. Children are to honor their parents; this involves obedience, and later friendship, and later caring for parents in their old age. Parents are to care for their children and help them to grow up into caring and responsible adults; later on, they are to provide emotional support for their grownup children through life's difficulties. There also are duties to brothers and sisters, and to members of an extended family. All these duties could be based on Ross's benevolence, nonmaleficence, and fidelity, or on a rule utilitarian view that seeks to promote the goods of family life.

Other social units, besides the family, include companies, schools, clubs, cities, and countries. Membership in a community brings special duties. Especially important is the duty to do your part to support the community and to make it better (including more just).

The next group gives duties that we have to anyone. We are not to kill, steal, or lie. Other duties are to show respect and politeness toward others, not enslave or insult them, help those in need, and show gratitude and reparation. In general, we are to do good and not harm to others. We are to treat others only in ways we consent to ourselves being treated in like circumstances.

The last group gives duties to ourselves. The duty not to covet is the duty to avoid bad desires, whether these be to steal or commit adultery (or to kill or lie or hate). Other duties to ourselves include self-improvement, self-regard, and future-regard. Perhaps the most important duty to ourselves is to live out our lives in the wisest way that we can.

These thoughts try to combine some insights from the philosophical and the Biblical traditions. You might try the same exercise yourself. What do you see as our main duties toward God, family, society, anyone, and ourselves?

11.6 Virtues and rights

Normative ethics deals with various big questions – such as:

1. What are the basic principles of right and wrong?
2. What things are ultimately worthwhile in life?
3. What would a just society be like?
4. What makes someone a good person?
5. What are the basic human rights?

We've focused mostly on question 1, but we also considered question 2 (hedonism versus pluralism) and 3 (distributive justice). Before finishing this chapter, I'd like to say a few very general things about virtues (question 4) and rights (question 5).

What makes someone a good person? Basically, to be a good person is to live in the right way and for the right reasons. The ancient Greeks emphasized four cardinal virtues:

- *wisdom:* rationally understanding how we ought to live.
- *courage:* facing danger and fear with proper confidence.
- *temperance:* having reason control our emotions.
- *justice:* dealing fairly with others.

To these natural virtues, Christianity added three theological virtues – and claimed that the greatest of these is love:

- *faith:* believing in God and in what he has revealed.
- *hope:* emotionally trusting in God and in his promises.
- *love:* unselfishly striving to serve God, and to do good and not harm to his creatures.

We've indirectly talked about three of these virtues – wisdom (forming our moral beliefs wisely and rationally), justice (impartiality and distributive justice), and love (the golden rule). But we talked about them in a different way. The virtue approach focuses on them as character traits rather than as principles of action.

In general, a **virtue** is a good habit – a disposition to act and feel in certain ways, a disposition that corresponds with and internalizes a correct principle of action. A good person is a virtuous person.

Virtues raise many of the same issues that we dealt with earlier. For example, how do we decide what is virtuous? Could we rationally argue with a Nazi who thinks that it's virtuous to persecute Jews? Does virtue depend on cultural standards? Or does it depend on God's will or self-evident truths? Are virtues just character traits that tend to maximize good consequences? How do *moral* virtues differ from virtues of other sorts? And how exactly does virtue relate to duty?

Another area of normative ethics asks, "What are the basic human rights?" In general, a **right** is something that one can justifiably demand of others. If you have a right, then you can demand that others treat you in certain ways. Traditionally, legal rights are distinguished from human rights. A **legal right** is a right recognized by the governing body of one's society. For example, in a given society we might have a legal right to sell our slaves. A **human right**, on the other hand, is a right that we have (or *ought* to have) simply because we're human beings – and not because we belong to a specific society. For example, all people have the human right not to be enslaved.

Moral rights traditionally divide into negative rights and positive rights. A **negative right** is a right to not be interfered with in certain ways. The Declaration of Independence spoke of our right to life, liberty, and the pursuit of happiness. These are areas where others ought not to interfere. It's wrong to take away the life or freedom or happiness of another, even if doing so maximizes the social good. In contrast, a **positive right** is a right to certain goods that others can provide. When people speak of the "right to adequate housing," they're thinking that society ought somehow to insure that people have adequate housing.

Rights raise controversial issues. For example, how do we decide what rights we have? Must we go by what our culture tells us? Or should we follow personal feelings, God's will, or self-evident truths? Are there objective truths about rights, or does talk about rights just express feelings or imperatives? Could we rationally argue with a Nazi who denies that Jews should have the same rights as Germans? Are any rights absolute? Do we have positive rights – or just negative ones? Do animals have rights? Can we translate statements about rights into statements about duties?

Normative ethics is a big area. My purpose in this book isn't to resolve all the issues. My purpose, rather, is to introduce some of the main issues and to propose some rational ways to deal with them.

11.7   Chapter summary

Nonconsequentialism says that some kinds of action (such as breaking promises or killing the innocent) are wrong in themselves, and not just wrong because they have bad consequences. Such things may be exceptionlessly wrong, or may just have some independent moral weight against them.

Ross's prima facie view is a popular form of nonconsequentialism. It tries to avoid the extreme implications of the "exceptionless duties" view and utilitarianism. Ross focuses on our duty to keep promises. This duty doesn't hold in an exceptionless way, since it can be overridden by other duties. And yet it isn't just a rule of thumb that we can break whenever it has good consequences to do so. Instead, the duty to keep promises is an independent duty. It binds us, other things being equal, but may sometimes have to yield to other duties.

Ross's basic moral principles say that we ought, other things being equal, to do or not to do certain kinds of things. There are duties of fidelity, reparation, gratitude, justice, beneficence, self-improvement, and nonmaleficence. When these duties conflict, we have to weigh one duty against another and see which is stronger in the situation.

Nonmaleficence is stronger than beneficence; in general, it's not right to harm one person to help another or to promote social usefulness. Many of our duties are relational; we have a specific duty to a person X because of how X is related to us (as, for example, someone to whom we've made a promise).

Ross's prima facie view, even though much of it seems acceptable, has several weaknesses. First, it's vague when we apply it to specific moral issues (for example, about the morality of killing). Second, it needs a better justice principle. Third, its objections to exceptionless norms are rather simplistic; we could improve the view by adding insights from rule utilitarianism about the importance of strict principles.

Distributive justice is about how goods ought to be distributed in a society. Utilitarians say that we ought to maximize the total good, and that we'll generally do this better by spreading out wealth more equally. Rawls says that society ought to promote the equal distribution of wealth, except for inequalities that serve as incentives to benefit everyone. Nozick says that whatever you earn fairly is yours – and society has no right to take it away to redistribute wealth or help the poor. I argue that the golden rule would lead us closer to Rawls than to Nozick.

Our philosophical approach tries to give a complete list of our basic duties in abstract terms. In contrast, the ten commandments try to give the most important of our concrete duties, but without aiming at completeness. The philosophical and the Biblical lists fit together nicely and offer mutually enriching insights. Both lists can be based on the golden rule.

We've been focusing on duty – on the principles that we *ought* to live by. But normative ethics also deals with virtues and human rights. These areas raise many of the same issues and controversies.

11.8   Study questions

Write out the answers in your ethics folder. If you don't know an answer, go back to the section that deals with it.

1. What is nonconsequentialism? Do all nonconsequentialists believe in exceptionless duties?
2. What is a "prima facie" duty? Why did Ima Rossian think that promise-keeping is a prima facie duty, and not exceptionless? (11.1)
3. Why did Ima reject the utilitarian approach to promises?
4. On Ima's view, what is intrinsically good? (11.2)
5. On Ross's view, what are our basic duties? What should we do when our duties conflict?
6. Explain Ross's intuitionism method. Did Ima accept this?
7. Explain the claim that nonmaleficence is stronger than beneficence.
8. Explain the claim that many of our duties are relational.
9. Does Ross's approach give us a definite answer to most moral questions? Give an example where it wouldn't.
10. Write about a page sketching your initial reaction to Ross's prima facie view. Does it seem plausible to you? What do you like and dislike about it? Can you think of any way to show that it's false?
11. What are the three objections to exceptionless norms? How could these be answered? (11.3)
12. What principle is suggested about how strictly to take a norm?
13. What is utilitarianism's approach to distributive justice? Explain how "diminishing marginal utility" tends to favor equality. (11.4)
14. Explain how Rawls proposes to pick out principles of justice. What is his "difference" principle?
15. What is the "entitlement view" of Robert Nozick? What is the golden rule argument for rejecting this approach?
16. How does our list of philosophical duties differ from the duties listed in the ten commandments? (11.5)
17. What is a virtue? What four basic virtues were recognized in ancient Greece? (11.6)
18. Distinguish between negative rights and positive rights. Sketch a couple of important issues about rights.

11.9 For further study

To solidify your understanding, do the computer exercises for "Ethics 11 – Nonconsequentialism." The Computer Exercises appendix at the end of this book has further information on this and on Internet resources.

Ross's view is in Chapter 2 of his *The Right and the Good*. Kant's *Groundwork of the Metaphysics of Morals* is the classic defense of an exceptionless-rules form of nonconsequentialism. For more on distributive justice and human rights, see Rawls's *A Theory of Justice* (his preface suggests which parts to read) and Nozick's *Anarchy, State and Utopia* (especially Chapter 7). The ten commandments are in Exodus 20:2–17 and Deuteronomy 5:6–21; any Bible has these. Aristotle's *The Nichomachaen Ethics* is a classic treatment of virtue; MacIntyre's *After Virtue* is an influential recent treatment. The Bibliography at the end of the book has information on how to find these works.

CHAPTER 12
Synthesis Chapter

CHAPTER 12
Synthesis Chapter

W e've studied various approaches to ethics. In this, our final chapter, we'll try to achieve a more unified understanding of these views and what difference they make. We'll do this by applying them to a specific moral issue – the hotly disputed topic of abortion. This will also be an example of *applied normative ethics*.

We'll first consider some abortion arguments that appeal to antecedent moral principles. Then we'll move back to our central question: "How should we pick out our moral principles?" I'll argue that the appeal to consistency gives a helpful way to deal with the issue.

12.1 Nonconsequentialism

Let's assume for the moment that it's *seriously wrong* to kill innocent human life. I'll take "seriously wrong" here to imply, at the very least, that killing wouldn't be justified to prevent a financial burden or an interference with one's job or schooling. Given this assumption, we can argue against abortion as follows:

> Killing innocent human life is seriously wrong.
> A fetus is innocent human life.
> ∴ Killing a fetus is seriously wrong.

Is the second premise true? Is a fetus human life? Many people assume that the whole issue depends on this question. If a fetus is human life, then abortion is wrong; otherwise, it's permissible.

However, many who are anti-abortion claim that a fetus isn't human life, but only *potential* human life; but they add that it's seriously wrong to kill potential human life. And many who are pro-abortion admit that the fetus is "human life" – but only in a trivial and irrelevant sense of the term; they say that the serious duty not to kill *human life* requires a stronger sense of the term and doesn't apply to the unborn. So they point to an ambiguity in the word "human."

When people disagree about whether a fetus is human life, what is the nature of this disagreement? Do both sides use the same sense of "human" – and differ only on whether a fetus is *human* in this sense? I think not. Instead, both sides use the word "human" differently. "Human" has at least three senses:

> **hu·man** (hyo͞o′mən) *n.* **1.** A born or unborn member of the species *Homo sapiens* **2.** A born member of the species *Homo sapiens* **3.** An animal who reasons

We use sense 1 in the biology lab when we distinguish between a "mouse fetus" and a "human fetus." We use sense 2 when we do a population study and count the number of humans in a city. Sense 3 is the traditional definition used to distinguish humans from other animals by their higher mental powers. A fetus is "human" in sense 1, but not in senses 2 or 3. So whether a fetus is "human" depends on which sense of "human" we use. "Is the fetus *human* life?" has a clear answer if we say what sense of "human" we're using in the question.

People have claimed human life to begin at various points:

(c) conception.
(i) individuation: when a zygote can't split or fuse with another.
(w) brain waves: when the fetus exhibits brain waves.
(v) viability: when the fetus could live apart.
(b) birth.
(r) rationality: when the child first thinks rationally.

Here we don't have a factual dispute over when there emerges, in the same clear sense of the term, a "human." Instead, we have six ways to use the ambiguous term "human."

The real issue is this: Which sense of "human" should we use when we say "Killing innocent *human* life is seriously wrong"? We get different principles depending on which sense we pick. If we use the neutral term "actual or potential human being" to cover any point from conception to adulthood, and thus avoid the verbal ambiguities, we can express the six principles as follows:

> It's seriously wrong to kill an innocent actual or potential human being, starting from the point of:
>
> (c) conception.   (w) brain waves.   (b) birth.
> (i) individuation.   (v) viability.   (r) rationality.

Principle (c) says that abortion at any point is seriously wrong. Principles (i), (w), and (v) permit earlier abortions but forbid later ones. Principle (b) permits any abortion but forbids infanticide. Principle (r) permits both abortion and infanticide. Which of the six should we accept?

Science can't decide the issue. Science can tell us whether an individual shows brain waves, and thus is "human" in sense (w). But it can't tell us which sense of "human" to use in our moral principle.

Most people pick the principle that fits their moral intuitions. This leads to an impasse, or stalemate, since people have different intuitions. Catholics were taught to oppose infanticide and abortion; their intuitions tend toward principle (c). Ancient Romans were brought up to allow both infanticide and abortion; their intuitions tend toward (r). Many today are taught to accept abortion but not infanticide; their intuitions tend to favor (b). So appealing to intuitions brings an impasse. To resolve the issue rationally, we need to appeal to something more basic.

Let's for the moment suppose that the serious duty not to kill begins at some point or other. To be concrete, let's suppose that it begins at birth. What about beings prior to this point? Do those who aren't yet born have:

1. no right to life at all,
2. a lesser but constant right to life, or
3. a gradually increasing right to life?

On option 1, a human fetus has *no* right to life. So killing it is permissible for minor reasons, or even no reason at all. On option 2, a fetus of any age has the same weak right to life, and can be killed for the same reasons. On option 3, the right to life gradually increases. So it's more seriously wrong (and requires more justification) to kill a fetus who is six months old than one who is three months old. Which of these options is the most plausible? Few people have firm moral intuitions about this. So again, appealing to moral intuitions won't lead to any firm conclusion. We need a better way to argue about moral principles.

So there are many possible nonconsequentialist norms about abortion. And we have yet to consider consequentialist views.

12.2 Consequentialism

Classical utilitarianism has a single basic norm: we ought always to do whatever maximizes the balance of pleasure over pain for everyone affected by our action. Here there's no special "right to life" that begins at some specific point; our only duty is to maximize good consequences. So we ask, "Will killing this fetus (or infant) maximize the balance of pleasure over pain?" If the answer is "yes," then we ought to kill.

Many who are pro-abortion argue on consequentialist grounds. They claim that abortions often have the best consequences. An abortion can avoid the disgrace to an unwed mother, the disruption of schooling or a career, and financial burdens. The child-to-be has less chance for happiness when these problems or probable birth defects exist. And abortion provides a second chance to prevent a birth when contraceptives fail.

Opponents say that we can have equally good results without abortion; we need better social support toward unwed mothers and poor families, better adoption practices, wiser use of contraceptives, artificial wombs, and so on. Children born with handicaps can lead happy and productive lives, if we show them love; such handicaps can bring families together and give them a sense of purpose. And abortions can harm women psychologically and promote callous attitudes toward human life.

Others object that we can't really know whether having or not having the baby would produce better consequences. We mostly rely on guesses when we apply utilitarianism.

More importantly, classical utilitarianism is a very questionable view. It justifies killing innocent humans (including the sick, handicapped, and elderly) when this produces even a tiny increase in good consequences. It has bizarre implications and is difficult to hold consistently. I argued in Chapter 10 that rationality would lead us to reject this approach.

In light of these problems, many have moved to rule utilitarianism with a pluralistic approach to values. Rule utilitarians would ask what rule about killing (including abortion) would have the best consequences for society to adopt and try to follow. One can plausibly argue that the rule with the best consequences would be a strict rule against killing (including against abortion).

Let's consider four rules about killing that society might adopt.

1. Killing innocent human life is permissible whenever this maximizes the balance of pleasure over pain.

Adopting this norm would have disastrous effects on society. Imagine what it would be like if your friends and relatives felt authorized to kill whenever they speculated that killing would have the best consequences. People would apply this in irresponsible ways, and respect for life would diminish. A rule against killing needs to be firm and definite.

2.   Killing a child is permissible until it exercises rationality.

This norm is extremely vague. When does a child reach the "point of rationality"? Does this happen when it first begins to speak, or when it enters the first grade, or when it graduates from high school? Since children develop gradually in their rational powers, it's arbitrary to pick a "point of rationality" at which it becomes wrong to kill children. Again, a rule against killing needs to be firm and definite. A vague rule like this would lead to a large amount of killing and would erode respect for human life at all levels.

3.   Killing a fetus is permissible, but killing an infant is wrong.

This norm is clearer (except for partial-birth abortions), but unstable. A late fetus and a newborn infant are practically identical except for their spatial location. So it will seem arbitrary to permit killing a late fetus but forbid killing a newborn. So societies that adapt this norm will tend to move toward accepting infanticide – and thus to norm 2 (with all its problems). Rules (i), (v), and (w) of the previous section would have similar instability problems.

4.   Killing innocent human life is seriously wrong, starting from
     the moment of conception.

This last norm, by contrast, gives clear guidelines and upholds respect for human life. A society that followed it would likely live better (in terms of long-range consequences) than a society that followed the other rules. So, one might argue, rule utilitarianism would seem to favor a strict rule against abortion.

12.3   Metaethical views

The last two sections considered various principles about abortion. Should we follow one of the nonconsequentialist principles? Or should we go with classical or rule utilitarianism?

We need to move to the more basic question: "How should we pick out our moral principles?" So we'll now consider the metaethical views that we studied earlier. First we'll listen to the Ima characters explain how they approach abortion. Then we'll turn to the GR consistency view, which I think gives a better way to deal with the issue.

Ima Relativist: "Morality is about social conventions; so our moral beliefs have to be based on what our society approves of. Now surveys show that most people in our society are moderately anti-abortion; they disapprove of most abortions, but allow some exceptions. So this should also be our view."

Ima Subjectivist: "A moral judgment is a statement about your feelings. When you consider a moral issue, about abortion or anything else, you have to go with how you feel. There's no 'objective truth' about whether abortion is right or wrong. Nor is there any effective way to reason about it. I can only suggest that you think about the issue and then see how you feel."

Ima Emotivist: "I basically agree with Ima Subjectivist. You have to go with your feelings."

Ima Idealist: "A moral judgment is a statement about what we'd feel if we were *rational*. Being rational involves things like being informed, impartial, and consistent. Consistency may give a way to resolve the issue. The next section talks about this."

Ima Supernaturalist: "Right and wrong are based on God's will. To discover God's will about abortion, I suggest that we look to the Bible and to the church.

"While the Bible doesn't mention the issue directly, I feel that it would lead one to be against abortion. It says much about loving your neighbor, and being concerned for the weak and defenseless. It says 'Thou shalt not kill.' And Psalm 139:13 and Jeremiah 1:5 speak of how God lovingly forms us in our mother's womb. When I pray about these passages and ask God for direction, I feel strongly that abortion is wrong. But I admit that other Christians who read the Bible and pray about it may come to the opposite conclusion.

"Church tradition from the beginning has condemned abortion. The *Didache*, which summarizes the teachings of the apostles, is one of the earliest Christian sources after the Bible. Here are verses 1:2 and 2:2 – which start with the law of love and the golden rule, and end by condemning abortion and infanticide:

> First, love the God who made you; secondly, your neighbor as yourself: do not do to another what you do not wish to be done to yourself.... Do not kill a fetus by abortion, or commit infanticide.

Catholic teaching has strongly condemned abortion. Many other (but not all) religious groups agree with this."

Ima Intuitionist: "There is an objective truth about the morality of abortion. To find this truth, we need to appeal to our moral intuitions. However, the apparent problem here is that people's intuitions about abortion vary widely. But maybe we can appeal to some very basic and widely shared intuitions (perhaps about consistency) to help us to think through the issue more clearly."

Ima Prescriptivist: "Moral judgments are prescriptions (or imperatives), not truth claims. But their logical structure gives us a way to reason about moral issues, like abortion, by appealing to consistency and the golden rule. The next section talks about how to do this."

12.4   GR consistency

Chapters 7 to 9 sketched a practical approach to moral rationality. This approach gives moral consistency principles that can be defended from various perspectives (as based on social conventions, personal feelings, God's will, self-evident truths, or whatever). These consistency principles require that we be impartial (make similar evaluations about similar actions, regardless of the individuals involved) and conscientious (keep our actions, resolutions, and desires in harmony with our moral beliefs). From these, we derived this golden rule theorem:

GR Theorem:	GR forbids this combination:
Treat others only as you consent to being treated in the same situation.	• I do something to another. • I'm unwilling that this be done to me in the same situation.

We proposed that we're *rational* in our moral judgments to the extent that we're consistent, informed, imaginative, and a few more things – where consistency includes impartiality, conscientiousness, and the golden rule. We used this approach to reason about racism and to attack racist moral beliefs.

I believe that this same approach forces us into an anti-abortion view. I'll argue that people of fairly normal desires won't, if they're consistent, hold that aborting a fetus is normally permissible.

Let me start with a parallel argument about stealing:

> If you're consistent and think that stealing is normally
> permissible, then you'll consent to the idea of others
> stealing from you in normal circumstances.
> You don't consent to the idea of others stealing from
> you in normal circumstances.
> ∴ If you're consistent, then you won't think that stealing
> is normally permissible.

The first premise is a golden rule consistency condition; it's somewhat like our GR theorem, and can be justified the same way. I'll assume that the second premise, about your desires, is true – that you aren't willing that people steal from you in normal circumstances. The conclusion is about the consistency of your holding a given moral belief. You can escape the conclusion if you don't care if people steal from you; this would make the second premise false. Through the rest of this chapter, I'll assume that you (the reader) desire not to be robbed or blinded or killed. If you don't care whether people do such things to you, then most of my further conclusions won't apply to you.

I think we can apply a similar argument to abortion. But let's go slowly on this. Let's first see if it makes sense to apply GR consistency to how we treat a fetus in a case that doesn't involve abortion.

Suppose that you're a pregnant woman. You're about to do some very heavy drinking, which you realize may harm the health of the unborn. But you ask yourself, "How do I react to the idea of my mother having done heavy drinking while pregnant with me?" If you do this to the unborn, and yet aren't willing that your mother would have done the same thing in similar circumstances while pregnant with you, then you violate the golden rule and are inconsistent. This use of the golden rule toward the unborn seems to make perfect sense. However, there are two things that we have to be careful about.

First, we need to ask about our present attitude toward a hypothetical case (see Section 8.2). We should ask, "How do I now (as an adult) react to the idea of my mother having done heavy drinking while pregnant with me?" We shouldn't ask about what desires we'd have if we were a fetus. Presumably a fetus has only very simple desires; it doesn't know much about alcohol and its possible harmful effects. So GR is about our present desires – about the fact that we now (as an adult) don't consent to the idea of our mother having done such drinking while pregnant with us.

Second, our question may raise worries about the human identity of the fetus. Someone may object as follows:

"I'm supposed to ask, 'How do I react to the idea of my mother having done heavy drinking while pregnant with *me*?' But doesn't this question presuppose that the fetus and my present self are identical – the same human being? So aren't you presupposing that the fetus is 'human'?"

If my wording presupposes this, we could change the wording. We could phrase the question in either of these ways:

- "How do I react to the idea of my mother having done heavy drinking while pregnant with the fetus that developed into my present self?"
- "How do I react to the idea of my mother having done heavy drinking while pregnant in the spring of 1945?" (Substitute some time a few months before your birth.)

These don't presuppose that the fetus and my present self are identical, or the "same human being." If you wish, you may rephrase what I say in one of these two ways. I'm against the idea of the heavy drinking, not because I think that the fetus was in some metaphysical sense the same human being as I, but because this drinking could have had harmful effects on me during my whole life.

Let's consider a more extreme example. Suppose again that you're a pregnant woman. But this time you're very sadistic. You're thinking of injecting yourself with a special blindness drug. The drug wouldn't affect you, but will cause your child to be born blind and remain blind all its life. You could inject the drug at various points in the pregnancy:

(c)   just after conception,
(i)   just after individuation,
(w)   when the fetus begins to have brain waves,
(v)   when the fetus becomes viable, or
(b)   just before birth.

However, at any of these points you'd violate the golden rule – since you aren't willing that your mother would have done this to you in a similar case. The moment of the injection is irrelevant, since the effect would be the same – you'd be blind all your life.

Applying the golden rule to abortion is similar. We only need to switch from a blindness drug (which blinds the fetus) to a death-drug (which kills it). Suppose that you're a pregnant woman. You're about to abort the fetus. But you ask yourself, "How do I react to the idea of my mother having aborted me under such circumstances?" If you kill the unborn, and yet don't consent to the idea of your mother having done the same thing to you in the same situation, then you violate the golden rule and are inconsistent.

As with the blinding case, the moment of the abortion (whether it happened, for example, just after conception or just before birth) makes little or no difference to our reaction. We're equally against the idea of ourselves having been aborted, regardless of the moment that we imagine the abortion having taken place, since the effect would be the same – we would never have been born.

We can argue as we did in the stealing case:

> If you're consistent and think that abortion is normally permissible, then you'll consent to the idea of your having been aborted in normal circumstances.
> You don't consent to the idea of your having been aborted in normal circumstances.
> ∴ If you're consistent, then you won't think that abortion is normally permissible.

Again, with most people the second premise will be true. Most people won't consent to (or approve of) the idea of this act having been done to them. So insofar as most people take a consistent position, they won't think abortion is normally permissible.

12.5 Some questions

> (Q1) Suppose that I approve of abortion but not infanticide or the blindness drug. Couldn't I consent to the idea of my having been aborted under actual or imagined normal circumstances, and so be consistent?

You could be consistent, but only with bizarre desires about how you yourself are to be treated. Suppose you hold these two principles:

1. It's wrong to blind an adult or child or infant or fetus.
2. It's wrong to kill an adult or child or infant, but it's right to kill a fetus.

To be consistent about your blinding principle 1, you'd have to answer these questions as follows:

- Do you consent to the idea of my blinding you now? – No!
- Do you consent to the idea of my having blinded you yesterday? – No!
- ... when you were five years old? – No!
- ... when you were five days old? – No!
- ... just before you were born? – No!

Similarly, to be consistent about your killing principle 2, you'd have to answer these questions as follows:

- Do you consent to the idea of my killing you now? – No!
- Do you consent to the idea of my having killed you yesterday? – No!
- ... when you were five years old? – No!
- ... when you were five days old? – No!
- ... just before you were born? – **Yes!**

It's strange that you disapprove equally of being blinded at the various times – and disapprove equally of being killed at the *first four* times – and yet approve of being killed at the *last* time. You oppose the blindings because, regardless of their timing, the effect would be the same – you'd be blind. You oppose the killings at the first four times because, again, the effect would be the same: you wouldn't be alive. But killing at the fifth time has the same effect. Why shouldn't you oppose this killing too? The "yes" here seems strange. So a person, to be consistent in holding the two principles, would have to have bizarre desires.

We can test our judgments about moral relevance by appealing to GR consistency. Maybe society taught us that dark skin merits abuse; so it's all right to abuse people with dark skin, but not people with white skin. To test this, we ask how we react to the idea of ourselves being abused in cases where we are white and in cases where we are dark. From this GR perspective, we see that skin color is morally irrelevant; we oppose our being abused regardless of what skin color we imagine ourselves having.

Similarly, we might have been taught that the point of birth (or viability, or whatever) is morally relevant to whether it's right to kill. To test this, we again ask how we react to the idea of ourselves having been killed before or after reaching this point. From the GR perspective, we see that the point is morally irrelevant. We're equally opposed to our having been killed at any point. Whether we'd be killed before or after reaching the point of birth (or viability, or whatever) makes little difference. So GR consistency leads us to think that killing is seriously wrong, starting from the moment of conception.

> (Q2) Are you saying that the desires that most people have are good, while unusual (or "bizarre") desires are bad? How would you establish this?

I'm not saying that common desires are good while unusual desires are bad. Often the reverse is true; and sometimes a conflict between our moral beliefs and our desires leads us to change our desires instead of our moral beliefs.

I'm appealing to desires that most people have because I'm arguing that most people who are pro-abortion are inconsistent. I'm challenging such people: "Look at what you'd have to desire in order to be consistent in your position – think about it and see whether you're consistent." I claim that most people who favor abortion support moral principles about the treatment of others that they're not willing to have had followed toward themselves.

> (Q3) If it would have been wrong for your parents to have aborted you, wouldn't it have been wrong for them not to have conceived you? The result would be the same – you wouldn't exist. So if abortion is wrong, then isn't it also wrong not to conceive children?

No, the cases differ in important (but complicated) ways.

My first reaction is to think that it would have been wrong for my parents not to have conceived me. But then I'd have to hold (since my case isn't special) that in general it's wrong not to conceive. In other words, I'd have to hold that everyone ought to conceive as much as possible. But I can't will this, since it would bring disaster to the world. So, to be consistent, I change my first reaction. I come to think that it would have been permissible for my parents not to have conceived me (but perhaps to have conceived someone else a month later).

Abortion doesn't raise the same problem, since I can easily hold that abortion in general is wrong. I can will a general prohibition against aborting, but not one against not-conceiving.

> (Q4) Suppose that reason forces us to think that abortion is wrong in *normal* cases. What does "normal" here mean? And aren't the "abnormal" cases the more important ones? So isn't your conclusion unimportant?

By "normal" here I mean "ordinary" or "typical." I mean to exclude cases where, for example, the life of the mother would be threatened, the baby would be grossly defective, or the pregnancy was caused by rape. I make this restriction because my way of reasoning doesn't always yield a definite answer for such cases.

Some people are willing that they would have been aborted under some unusual conditions. Suppose that the baby would be born severely handicapped; some might prefer not to have lived at all than to live in this condition. Or suppose that the baby would die within a week after its birth; here one might easily consent to having been aborted.

In both these cases, I personally think that an abortion would be wrong. Because I see our lives in a larger religious context, I see *every* life as worth living; so I have trouble willing my abortion under any circumstances. But my way of reasoning doesn't by itself (apart from the religious context) force this conclusion.

If my arguments work, reason forces the conclusion that abortion is wrong *at least normally* (in the great majority of cases) – and *seriously wrong* (since I can't will my own non-existence for small reasons). But it leaves some details fuzzy. This is how reason usually works in ethics. For example, reason forces the conclusion that racism in general is wrong (see Sections 7.4 and 9.3). But it doesn't give as decisive an answer about the details (on bussing, quotas, ways to combat racism, and so on). It would be nice if reason were powerful enough to eliminate all the gray areas; but I don't see any way to do this. I'm happy, instead, that reason is powerful enough to make *many* things in ethics fairly clear.

Does this concession make my general conclusion about abortion unimportant? I think not. On the contrary, in light of the great number of "convenience abortions" going on, the general moral status of abortion is now the more important issue. So it's very important if, without presupposing any antecedent moral premises (except ones about consistency), we can show that the rational approach to abortion is to hold that it's seriously wrong in at least the great majority of cases.

> (Q5) What should I do if I'm not 100% convinced of your argument against abortion?

If there's genuine doubt in your mind about the morality of abortion, you ought to take the safer course – and not do what genuinely might be seriously wrong.

Suppose that you have a revolver in your hand with some bullets, but you don't know how many. If you point the gun to someone's head and pull the trigger, it might go off or it might not. It would be wrong to pull the trigger if there's a genuine possibility that it might go off. Similarly, it would be wrong to have an abortion if there's a genuine possibility that it might be as evil to do this as to kill a five-year-old child.

(Q6) Why have you avoided the terms "pro-life" and "pro-choice"?

I prefer "anti-abortion" and "pro-abortion," since these terms are less emotional. Also, the "pro-choice" view isn't really about whether abortion is wrong. Instead, it's about whether abortion should be legal. Some who are pro-choice think that abortion is wrong but should be legal. While I disagree with this (and question the GR consistency of this view), I don't want to discuss it here.

Abortion raises a lot of complicated issues. My purpose here isn't to resolve all the issues. My purpose, rather, is to sketch a rational way to reason about the morality of abortion.

12.6   Chapter summary

This final synthesis chapter tries to promote a more unified understanding of the views that we've studied and what difference they make. It does this by applying the views to the controversial topic of abortion.

Some argue that abortion must be seriously wrong – since a fetus is innocent human life and it's seriously wrong to kill innocent human life. But "human" has various senses. A fetus is "human" in some of these senses, but not in others. The real issue is what sense of "human" we should use when we say "Killing innocent *human* life is seriously wrong." Depending on how we take "human," we get different principles – with different implications about when it's seriously wrong to kill.

Classical utilitarians argue that we ought to kill a fetus or infant whenever doing so has the best consequences; this would seem to favor the pro-abortion view. Rule utilitarians say that we ought to adopt whatever rule about killing (including abortion) would have the best consequences for society to adopt and try to live by; this would seem to favor the anti-abortion view.

Since these arguments all appeal to controversial moral premises, we moved to the more basic question: "How should we pick out our moral principles?" So we considered some of the main views on this – including cultural relativism, subjectivism, emotivism, the ideal observer view, supernaturalism, intuitionism, and prescriptivism.

The last two sections argue that golden rule consistency forces us into an anti-abortion view. It claims that most people won't be consistent if they hold that abortion is normally permissible – since they won't consent to the idea of themselves having been aborted in normal circumstances. But this argument, even if it succeeds at what it tries to do, still leaves some of the details fuzzy.

12.7 Study questions

Write out the answers in your ethics folder. If you don't know an answer, go back to the section that deals with it.

1. Suppose that we agree that killing innocent human life is seriously wrong. If we claim that a fetus isn't human life, how could we still be strongly anti-abortion? (12.1)

2. Suppose that we agree that killing innocent human life is seriously wrong. If we claim that a fetus is human life, how could we still be strongly pro-abortion?

3. What are some of the main senses of the word "human"? In which of these senses is the fetus "human"?

4. Can we decide what sense of "human" to use in the principle "Killing innocent *human* life is seriously wrong" by appealing to science? Can we decide by appealing to moral intuitions?

5. Explain and give objections to the classical utilitarian argument in favor of abortion. (12.2)

6. How would rule utilitarianism apply to abortion? How might one use this approach to argue against abortion?

7. How would cultural relativism, subjectivism, supernaturalism, and intuitionism apply to abortion? (12.3)

8. What is the GR consistency argument against stealing? (12.4)

9. Give an example of how to apply GR consistency to our treatment of a fetus in a case that doesn't involve abortion.

10. What is the GR consistency argument against abortion?

11. Could a person be consistent who disapproves of the blindness drug and infanticide – but who approves of abortion? What desires would such a person have to have? (12.5)

12. Explain why the GR argument doesn't yield a definite answer on some abortion cases.

13. Is the conclusion that abortion is "normally wrong" unimportant – since it avoids the tricky question of what unusual situations, if any, would justify abortion?

14. What does this book say we should do if we're still unsure about the morality of abortion?

15. Is being pro-choice the same as being pro-abortion?

12.8 For further study

To solidify your understanding, do the computer exercises for "Ethics 12 – Synthesis Chapter." The Computer Exercises appendix at the end of this book has further information on this and on Internet resources.

Many of the ideas in this chapter are adapted from Gensler's "A Kantian argument against abortion." This article also discusses two further influential articles defending abortion: Thomson's "A defense of abortion" and Tooley's "Abortion and infanticide." Hare also wrote an article on "Abortion and the golden rule"; but his approach was significantly different from mine. For the *Didache* reference, see Kleist 1948. For a thorough defense of the anti-abortion view, see Schwarz's *The Moral Question of Abortion*. The Bibliography at the end of the book has information on how to find these works; the reference to the Gensler article mentions two books with further readings on abortion.

APPENDIX

Computer Exercises

Various computer tools go with this book. These include computer exercises, related Web links, and resources for teachers. I suggest that you go to one of the five sections of this appendix depending on which condition applies:

Go to this section:	If this applies:
A. Getting the software	You want to get the exercise software from the Internet.
B. Disk-based exercises	Your teacher gave you a disk with the exercise software.
C. Web exercises	You want to do the exercises on your Web browser.
D. Web links	You want to pursue related Web sites on ethics.
E. Teacher resources	You're a teacher and would appreciate some help.

A.   Getting the software

Each chapter in this book has computer exercises with multiple-choice questions. These are an effective and enjoyable tool for learning.

This section tells you how to get the latest Windows and DOS versions of the exercise software from the Internet Web. If you already have this software on a disk, go instead to Section B. If you'd prefer to do the exercises directly on your Web browser, go instead to Section C.

To get the exercise software, first start your Web browser (usually Netscape or Internet Explorer). Then go to either of these addresses:

http://www.routledge.com/routledge/philosophy/cip/ethics.htm
http://www.jcu.edu/philosophy/gensler/ethics.htm

The first address is the Routledge site on this book; the second address is my personal page. Both Web sites should have the same book materials. If neither address works, try a Web search for "Gensler's Philosophy Exercises."

My Web page starts like this:

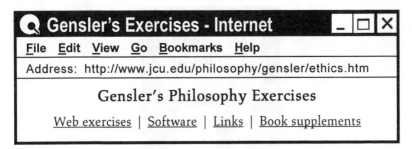

Click "<u>Software</u>" with your mouse. Then the screen will look like this:

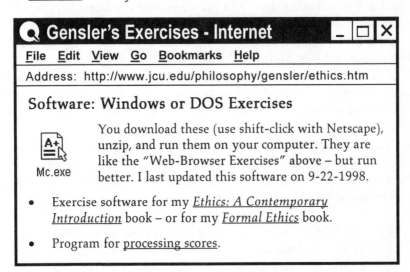

With Netscape, hold down the shift key and click the first underlined book title. With Internet Explorer, click the underlined title with the *right* mouse button and then pick "Save Target As." In both cases, you have to specify what folder you want to put the file in. If all goes well, the file ET-INTRO.ZIP will be copied to your hard disk. Unzip this file resulting files (minus ET-INTRO.ZIP, which you can erase) to a floppy disk. This gives you a disk with the ethics exercises that you can run on a personal computer. The next section tells how to use this disk.

B. Disk-based exercises

This section assumes that you want to do the disk-based exercises. You have an ethics disk that looks something like this, and you want to know how to use it:

If you don't have such a disk, you can download the latest version of the same exercise software from the Internet Web (see Section A above). Or you might prefer to do the same exercises on your Web browser, directly from the Internet (see Section C below).

To run the disk-based ethics program, you need an IBM-compatible personal computer. Your disk has two versions of the ethics program: one for Windows and one for DOS. The two have the same exercises but start up in different ways.

To start the *Windows version* of the ethics program, first start Windows; you normally do this by just turning on the computer and waiting for the screen to settle down. Then put your ethics disk in drive A. Bring up the Run Box in one of these ways:

1.   If you see a Start Button, point to it with your mouse and click the left mouse button. Then point to the word "Run" with your mouse and click again.

2.   If you see a Program Manager window, point to the word "File" in its menubar with your mouse and click the left mouse button. Then point to the word "Run" with your mouse and click again.

3.   If you see neither of the above, then hold down these two keys simultaneously: CTRL + ESC (⌨⌨). You'll then see the Start Button, or a task manager that leads to the Program Manager.

In the Run Box, type "A:ETHICS" (without quotes) and click "OK" (or hit the ENTER key ⌨). If your ethics disk only fits drive B, then type "B:ETHICS" instead. After a few seconds, the program should start.

The *DOS version* of the program is for older computers that don't run Windows. To start the DOS version, first start DOS. With an older computer, you normally do this by just turning on the computer and waiting for the screen to settle down. If you see a DOS prompt on the screen that looks something like this (with "_" flashing on and off) then you're all set:

(If you don't see this DOS prompt, ask someone how to get it; if you see little pictures instead, then you're probably in Windows and can follow the previous directions for starting the Windows version.) When you see this DOS prompt, type "A:ETH" (without quotes):

Then hit the ENTER key ⌨. If your ethics disk only fits drive B, then type "B:ETH" instead. After a few seconds, the program should start.

If your teacher set up your disk to be self-booting, then you also can start the DOS version by just putting the disk in the computer and then turning on the computer.

If you have your own computer, you may want to put the program on your hard disk. Then you'll have to copy the SCORE.MC and MC.INI score files from your hard disk to a floppy disk when your teacher wants to record scores.

The ethics program starts with a welcome screen:

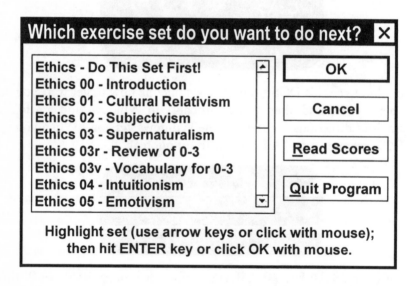

You'll be asked for your first and last name; give these carefully, because scores record under your name. After being asked about sound effects (keep them OFF if others may be disturbed), you'll see a list of exercises:

The set called "Ethics - Do This Set First!" is the one to do first, since it give you a further explanation of the program.

A typical exercise set begins with short summaries of key points. Then you get multiple-choice problems. When you finish, your score records to the disk. If you later do the set again and get a higher score, your higher score counts instead. Here's a sample problem:

```
┌─────────────────────────────────────────────────────────────┐
│ ▲⧉ Ethics 01 - Cultural Relativism        _ □ X │
├─────────────────────────────────────────────────────────────┤
│ File  Readings  Options  Help                                 │
├─────────────────────────────────────────────────────────────┤
│                                                               │
│  Cultural relativism holds that "Racism is wrong" means       │
│                                                               │
│      {1} I disapprove of racism.                              │
│      {2} My society disapproves of racism.                    │
│      {3} Racism doesn't maximize society's total happiness.   │
│                                                               │
│  What is your answer, Harry?                                  │
│                                                               │
│  ─────────────────                                            │
│                                                               │
│  TO ANSWER: point-&-click with your mouse, or type the        │
│  number, or highlight the number (using spacebar or up/down   │
│  arrow keys) & hit the ENTER key.                             │
│                                                               │
└─────────────────────────────────────────────────────────────┘
```

The directions are straightforward. When you give an answer, you'll get further feedback or explanations.

Apart from the "Ethics - Do This Set First!" set, there are four types of exercise set:

- Ethics 00 to 12 cover the Introduction and Chapters 1 to 12.
- Ethics 03r, 06r, 09r, and 12r review groups of chapters.
- Ethics 03v, 06v, 09v, and 12v cover vocabulary items.
- Ethics 06z, 09z, and 12z review the book up to a given point.

Your teacher may tell you what exercises to do and may specify a minimum score (perhaps 85% or 90%) that you need to get. If you complete an exercise set more than once, your highest score counts. It's good to keep repeating a set until you get almost everything right; that will give you a firmer grasp of the material. The review sets (those ending in "r" or "z," like "Ethics 03r") are very useful for preparing for an exam. These sets ask you random problems from several chapters and give a quick way to test your understanding of the material.

C.   Web exercises

Section B talks about the disk-based exercises for this book that you can run on a personal computer. You also can do the same exercises on your Web browser directly from the Internet, instead of from a disk.

Using your Web browser, go to either of these addresses:

http://www.routledge.com/routledge/philosophy/cip/ethics.htm
http://www.jcu.edu/philosophy/gensler/ethics.htm

If you have trouble, see the suggestions under Section A.

My Web page starts like this:

```
┌────────────────────────────────────────────────────────────┐
│ Q Gensler's Exercises - Internet          [ _ ][ □ ][ X ]   │
├────────────────────────────────────────────────────────────┤
│ File  Edit  View  Go  Bookmarks  Help                       │
├────────────────────────────────────────────────────────────┤
│ Address: http://www.jcu.edu/philosophy/gensler/ethics.htm   │
├────────────────────────────────────────────────────────────┤
│              Gensler's Philosophy Exercises                  │
│                                                              │
│    Web exercises | Software | Links | Book supplements       │
│  ────────────────────────────────────────────────────────   │
│                                                              │
│  Web Exercises                                               │
│                                                              │
│            Each exercise has a reading plus multiple-choice  │
│            problems. If the problems require scrolling, try to│
│            have your browser show more text: use a smaller   │
│            font, hide the toolbar, maximize the window, etc. │
│                                                              │
│  For my Ethics: A Contemporary Introduction book:            │
│                                                              │
│  1. Introduction | Cultural Relativism | Subjectivism |      │
│     Supernaturalism | Vocabulary                             │
│                                                              │
│  2. Intuitionism | Emotivism | Prescriptivism | Vocabulary   │
└────────────────────────────────────────────────────────────┘
```

Click the exercise that you want to do. A typical question looks like this:

```
┌────────────────────────────────────────────────────────────┐
│ Q Cultural Relativism - Internet          [ _ ][ □ ][ X ]   │
├────────────────────────────────────────────────────────────┤
│ File  Edit  View  Go  Bookmarks  Help                       │
├────────────────────────────────────────────────────────────┤
│ Address: http://www.jcu.edu/philosophy/gensler/ethics.htm   │
├────────────────────────────────────────────────────────────┤
│                   What is your answer?                       │
│                                                              │
│  Cultural relativism holds that "Racism is wrong" means      │
│                                                              │
│     {1}   I disapprove of racism.                            │
│     {2}   My society disapproves of racism.                  │
│     {3}   Racism doesn't maximize society's total happiness. │
│                                                              │
│            <= back | menu | forward =>                       │
│         Directions: Click on a number from 1 to 3.           │
└────────────────────────────────────────────────────────────┘
```

D.   Web links

The Internet Web is a great source of information about almost every-thing, including ethics. I collected various links to ethics sites that relate to this book. These sites can be particularly useful if you're writing a paper on a given topic.

You can go to these related ethics Web sites in two ways:

1.   If you're doing an exercise, you can go to these Web sites by clicking where it says to click. This works using both disk-based exercises (Section B) and Web exercises (Section C).
2.   If you're in either of the Web sites for this book (see Sections A or C), click the word "<u>Links</u>" at the top of the page. You'll go to the "Links to Related Sites" Section.

These sites have a wealth of information. For example, the Web sites for the synthesis chapter on abortion let you link to (a) two influential pro-abortion organizations (and their arguments defending abortion), (b) two influential anti-abortion organizations (and their arguments against abortion), (c) the complete text of a comprehensive book on abortion, and (d) a site with further links on virtually every aspect of abortion.

E.   Teacher resources

The Web sites for this book have various resources for teachers. If you're a teacher, you should check these out.

Using your Web browser (typically Netscape or Internet Explorer), go to either of these addresses:

http://www.routledge.com/routledge/philosophy/cip/ethics.htm
http://www.jcu.edu/philosophy/gensler/ethics.htm

If you have trouble, see the suggestions under Section A.

My Web page starts like this:

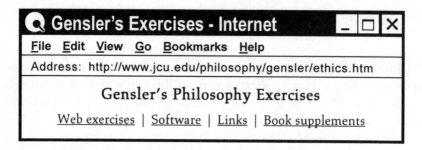

The last three links are of particular interest to teachers.

- If you click "<u>Software</u>," you'll go to a section where you can download the disk-based exercises for your students. You also can download a program for recording and processing student scores. See Sections A and B for further information.

- If you click "<u>Links</u>," you'll go to the "Links to Related Sites" Section where you can link to related ethics sites. See Section D for further information.

- If you click "<u>Book supplements</u>," you'll go to the "Book Supplements" Section. This has an on-line teacher's manual that talks about how to use the book and software in your courses. It may also include other things.

I invite teachers to send me items (like sample tests or handouts) to put in the "Book Supplements" Section.

Glossary

> This includes terms introduced in **bold type** in the text, plus a few other common terms. The reader should be warned that other authors may use some of these terms in somewhat different senses.

Act utilitarianism   We ought to do the ACT with the best consequences for everyone. (This contrasts with **rule utilitarianism**.)

Analytic statement   A statement that is true by definition. Equivalently, a statement that is true because of logical connections and the meaning of terms.

Applied normative ethics   Studying moral questions about specific areas, like abortion or lying.

Argument   A set of statements consisting of premises and a conclusion.

Beneficence   Do good to others.

Biting the bullet   Accepting an implausible consequence of your view.

Classical utilitarianism   We ought to do whatever maximizes the balance of pleasure over pain for everyone affected by our action.

Cognitivism   Moral judgments are truth claims, and so are literally true or false. (Examples of cognitivism include cultural relativism, subjectivism, the ideal observer view, supernaturalism, and intuitionism.)

Conscientiousness   Keep your actions, resolutions, and desires in harmony with your moral beliefs.

Consequentialism   We ought to do whatever maximizes good consequences.

Cultural relativism (CR)   "Good" means "socially approved." (This is sometimes called "ethical relativism" and is distinct from "descriptive relativism," which claims that different societies *in fact* disagree about basic moral norms.)

Deontological ethics   Any approach to normative ethics that denies that the rightness of an action depends on how it promotes intrinsically good consequences. See **nonconsequentialism**.

Descriptive relativism   See **cultural relativism**.

Difference principle   Society ought to promote the equal distribution of wealth, except for inequalities that serve as incentives to benefit everyone (including the least advantaged group) and are open to everyone on an equal basis.

Diminishing marginal utility of money The fact that, as we get richer, each extra dollar makes less difference to how well we live.

Divine command view See **supernaturalism**.

Egoism We ought to do whatever maximizes good consequences for ourselves. (This is sometimes called "ethical egoism" and is distinct from "psychological egoism," which claims that people always *in fact* do whatever they think will maximize good consequences for themselves.)

Emotivism "X is good" means "Hurrah for X!"

Empirical statement A statement that is testable by sense experience. Equivalently, a statement that can in principle be shown by our sense experience to be true or at least highly probable.

Ends–means consistency Keep your means in harmony with your ends.

Entitlement view of just possessions Whatever you earn fairly is yours – and society has no right to take it away from you in order to redistribute wealth or help the poor.

Equal liberty principle Society ought to safeguard the greatest liberty for each person compatible with an equal liberty for all others.

Ethics See **moral philosophy**.

Exactly similar acts Acts that have all the same properties in common.

Extrinsically good Whatever has good consequences. (This contrasts with **intrinsically good**.)

Fidelity Keep your promises.

First principle See **self-evident truth**.

Formula of universal law Act only as you're willing for anyone to act in the same situation – regardless of imagined variations of time or person.

Future-regard principle Don't do what you'll later regret. More precisely, treat yourself (in the future) only as you're willing to have been treated by yourself (in the past).

GR consistency condition This combination is logically inconsistent: (a) I believe that I *ought* to do something to another, and (b) I don't desire that this be done to me in the same situation.

GR theorem Treat others only as you consent to being treated in the same situation. More precisely, don't combine these two: (a) I do something to another, and (b) I'm unwilling that this be done to me in the same situation.

Gratitude Return good to those who have done good to you.

Hedonism Only pleasure is intrinsically good and only pain is intrinsically bad. (This is sometimes called "ethical hedonism" and is distinct from "psychological hedonism," which claims that people always *in fact* act only for the sake of gaining pleasure and avoiding pain.)

Hedonistic utilitarianism See **classical utilitarianism**.

Human right A right that we have (or ought to have) simply because we're human beings – and not because we're members of such and such a society.

Hume's law We can't deduce an "ought" from an "is." Equivalently, we need a moral premise to deduce a moral conclusion.

Ideal observer A person of ideal moral wisdom. Roughly, one who is fully informed and has impartial concern for everyone.

Ideal observer view (IO) "X is good" means "We'd desire X if we were fully informed and had impartial concern for everyone."

Impartiality Make similar evaluations about similar actions, regardless of the individuals involved.

Intrinsically good Whatever is good in itself, abstracting from further consequences. (This contrasts with **extrinsically good**.)

Intuitionism "Good" is indefinable, there are objective moral truths, and the basic moral truths are self-evident to a mature mind. (Some intuitionists prefer to say that basic moral truths, instead of being self-evident, are grasped by a kind of perception that resembles sense experience.)

Justice Treating others as they have a right to be treated. (See **right**.) Also, Ross's principle that we are to upset distributions of pleasure or happiness that don't accord with merit.

Legal right A right recognized by the governing body of the society that we live in.

Literal golden rule If you want X to do something to you, then do this same thing to X.

Logical positivism Any genuine truth claim is either empirical (testable by sense experience) or analytic (true by definition).

Logical reasoning Concluding something (the conclusion) from something else (the premises).

Logicality Avoid inconsistent beliefs.

Metaethics Studying the nature and methodology of moral judgments.

Moderate emotivism Moral judgments, while they express emotions and not truth claims, are rational to the extent that they are informed and impartial.

Moral philosophy Reasoning about the ultimate questions of morality. (The two main branches of moral philosophy are **metaethics** and **normative ethics**.)

Moral realism See **objective view of values**.

Natural right See **human right**.

Naturalism "Good" is definable using ideas from sense experience.

Negative right A right to not be interfered with in certain ways. (The right to free speech is an example; this is a right not to have our speech interfered with.)

Noncognitivism Moral judgments aren't truth claims, and so aren't literally true or false. (Examples of noncognitivism include emotivism and prescriptivism.)

Nonconsequentialism   Some kinds of action (such as killing the innocent) are wrong in themselves, and not just wrong because they have bad consequences.

Nonmaleficence   Don't harm others.

Normative ethics   Studying principles about how we ought to live. (Normative ethics looks for norms about what is right or wrong, virtuous, worthwhile, or just. The two main branches of normative ethics are **normative theory** and **applied normative ethics**.)

Normative theory   Studying very general moral principles.

Objective view of values   Some things are objectively right or wrong, independently of what anyone may think or feel.

Original position   A hypothetical situation where people are free, clearheaded, and know all the relevant facts – but don't know about their own place in society (whether rich or poor, black or white, male or female).

Philosophy   Reasoning about the ultimate questions of life.

Pluralism   Many things are intrinsically good (for example, virtue, knowledge, pleasure, life, and freedom).

Pluralistic rule utilitarianism   We ought to follow the RULES with the best consequences for society to follow – and we should evaluate consequences in terms of various goods, such as virtue, knowledge, pleasure, life, and freedom.

Positive right   A right to certain goods that others can provide. (The right to adequate housing is an example.)

Prescription   Imperative (like "Do this").

Prescriptivism   "You ought to do this" is a universalizable prescription; it means "Do this and let everyone do the same in similar cases."

Prima facie duty   A duty that holds if other things are equal. More precisely, a factor that tends in itself to make something our duty but can sometimes be over-ridden by other factors.

Prima facie view   The basic moral principles say that we ought, other things being equal, to do or not to do certain kinds of things.

Psychological egoism   See egoism.

Psychological hedonism   See hedonism.

Rationality condition   A principle stating how we *ought* (ideally) to form our moral beliefs.

Relevantly similar acts   Acts that are so similar that the reasons why one fits in a given moral category also apply to the others.

Reparation   Make up for any harm that you've done to another.

Right   Something that one can justifiably demand of others. See **legal right**, **human right**, **negative right**, and **positive right**.

Ross's prima facie view   See prima facie view.

Rule utilitarianism We ought to do what would be prescribed by the RULES with the best consequences for people in society to try to follow. (This contrasts with **act utilitarianism.**)

Self-evident truth A known truth that requires no further proof or justification.

Self-improvement Improve your virtue, knowledge, and so on.

Self-regard principle Treat yourself only as you're willing to have others treat themselves in the same situation.

Subjectivism (SB) "X is good" means "I like X."

Supernaturalism (SN) "X is good" means "God desires X."

Teleological ethics Any approach to normative ethics that affirms that the rightness of an action depends on how it promotes intrinsically good consequences. See **consequentialism.**

Truth claim A statement that is true or false.

Universalizability principle Whatever is right (wrong, good, bad, etc.) in one case would also be right (wrong, good, bad, etc.) in any exactly or relevantly similar case, regardless of the individuals involved.

Universalizable A judgment that logically commits us to making a similar judgment about similar cases.

Utilitarianism We ought to do whatever maximizes good consequences for everyone. See **act utilitarianism, classical utilitarianism, pluralistic rule utilitarianism,** and **rule utilitarianism.**

Valid argument An argument in which the conclusion follows logically from the premises. (For an argument to be "valid," the premises needn't be true; but proving something requires true premises.)

Virtue A good habit. More precisely, a disposition to act and feel in certain ways, a disposition that corresponds with and internalizes a correct principle of action.

Bibliography

Aquinas, St. Thomas, *Treatise on Law*, Chicago: Henry Regnery, 1970. This has questions 90–97 of part I–II (Prima Secundae) of the *Summa Theologica*.

Aristotle, *The Nichomachean* Ethics, trans. J.E.C. Welldon, Buffalo NY: Prometheus Books, 1987.

Ashby, R.W. (1967) "Verifiability principle," in the *Encyclopedia of Philosophy*.

Ayer, A.J. (1946) *Language, Truth and Logic*, New York: Dover.

Benedict, R. (1934) "A defense of cultural relativism," *The Journal of General Psychology*, 10: 59–82. Several anthologies have this essay, including C. Sommers (ed.), *Vice and Virtue in Everyday Life*, San Diego: Harcourt Brace Jovanovich, 1985.

Blackburn, S. (1993) *Essays in Quasi-Realism*, Oxford: Oxford University Press.

Brandt, R. (1953) "In search of a credible form of utilitarianism," in G. Nakhnikian and H. Castañeda (eds), *Morality and the Language of Conduct*, Detroit, Wayne State University Press.

—— (1955) "The definition of an 'ideal observer' theory in ethics" and "Some comments on Professor Firth's reply," *Philosophy and Phenomenological Research*, 15: 407–13 and 422–3.

—— (1959) *Ethical Theory*, Englewood Cliffs, NJ: Prentice-Hall.

—— (1967a) "Ethical relativism," in the *Encyclopedia of Philosophy*.

—— (1967b) "Happiness," in the *Encyclopedia of Philosophy*.

Cadoux, A.T. (1912) "The implications of the golden rule," *Ethics*, 3: 272–87.

Carson, T. (1984) *The Status of Morality*, Dordrecht: D. Reidel.

Darwin, C. (1839) *The Voyage of the Beagle*, New York: P.F. Collier, 1909.

Encyclopedia Britannica (1994-8) Britannica CD 98 Multimedia Edition, Chicago: Encyclopedia Britannica, Inc.

Encyclopedia of Ethics (1992) L. and C. Becker (eds), New York: Garland.

Encyclopedia of Philosophy (1967) P. Edwards (ed.), London and New York: Macmillan and the Free Press. The Supplement (D. Borchert, ed.) came out in 1996.

Firth, R. (1952) "Ethical absolutism and the ideal observer," *Philosophy and Phenomenological Research*, 12: 317–45. Brandt (1955) replied to this article, and Firth (1955) replied to Brandt.

—— (1955) "Reply to Professor Brandt," *Philosophy and Phenomenological Research*, 15: 414–21.
Frankena, W. (1966) "Two concepts of morality," *Journal of Philosophy*, 63: 688–96.
—— (1973) *Ethics*, Englewood Cliffs, NJ: Prentice-Hall, second edition.
Gensler, H. (1986) "A Kantian argument against abortion," *Philosophical Studies*, 49: 83–98. This was reprinted in R.M. Baird and S.E. Rosenbaum (eds), *The Ethics of Abortion*, Buffalo: Prometheus Books, 1989, and in L.P. Pojman and F.J. Beckwith (eds), *The Abortion Controversy*, Boston and London: Jones and Bartlett, 1995.
—— (1986) "Ethics is based on rationality," *Journal of Value Inquiry*, 20: 251–64.
—— (1989) *Logic: Analyzing and Appraising Arguments*, Englewood Cliffs, NJ: Prentice Hall.
—— (1996) *Formal Ethics*, London: Routledge.
Gibbard, A. (1990) *Wise Choices, Apt Feelings*, Cambridge, MA: Harvard University Press.
Haas, P.J. (1988) *Morality after Auschwitz*, Philadelphia: Fortress Press.
Hare, R.M. (1952) *The Language of Morals*, Oxford: Clarendon Press.
—— (1963) *Freedom and Reason*, Oxford: Clarendon Press.
—— (1975) "Abortion and the golden rule," *Philosophy and Public Affairs*, 4: 201–22.
—— (1981) *Moral Thinking*, Oxford: Clarendon Press.
Hertzler, J.O. (1934) "On golden rules," *Ethics*, 44: 418–36.
Hume, D. (1965) *Hume's Ethical Writings*, A. MacIntyre (ed.), London: Collier-Macmillan Ltd. This has selections from Hume's ethical works: *A Treatise of Human Nature* (1739) and *An Enquiry Concerning the Principles of Morals* (1751).
Johnson, O. (ed.) (1994) *Ethics: Selections from Classical and Contemporary Writers*, Fort Worth, Texas: Harcourt Brace College Publishers.
Kant, I. (1785) *Groundwork of the Metaphysics of Morals*, trans. H.J. Paton, New York: Harper & Row, 1964.
Kleist, J.A. (trans.) (1948) "The Didache," in J. Quasten and J.C. Plumpe (eds), *Ancient Christian Writers 6*, Westminster, MD: The Newman Press.
Kohlberg, L. (1972) "A cognitive-developmental approach to moral education," *Humanist*, 32: 13–16.
—— (1981 and 1984) *Essays on Moral Development* (*The Philosophy of Moral Development* and *The Psychology of Moral Development*), vols 1 and 2, San Francisco: Harper & Row.
MacIntyre, A. (1984) *After Virtue*, Notre Dame, IN: University of Notre Dame Press, second edition.
Mackie, J.L. (1977) *Ethics: Inventing Right and Wrong*, London: Penguin.
Mill, J.S. (1861) *Utilitarianism*, New York: Library of Liberal Arts, 1957.

Moore, G.E. (1903) *Principia Ethica*, Cambridge: Cambridge University Press.

Nielsen, K. (1967) "Ethics, problems of," in the *Encyclopedia of Philosophy*.

Nozick, R. (1974) *Anarchy, State and Utopia*, New York: Basic Books.

Ockham, W. (1957) *Philosophical Writings of William of Ockham*, trans. P. Boehner, Indianapolis, IN: Bobbs-Merrill.

Passmore, J. (1967a) "Logical positivism," in the *Encyclopedia of Philosophy*.

—— (1967b) "Philosophy," in the *Encyclopedia of Philosophy*.

Plato, *Euthyphro*. Several anthologies have this dialogue, including E. Hamilton and H. Cairns (eds), *The Collected Dialogues of* Plato, New York: Pantheon Books, 1963.

Quinn, P.L. (1978) *Divine Commands and Moral Requirements*, New York: Oxford University Press.

Rawls, J. (1971) *A Theory of Justice*, Cambridge: Harvard University Press.

Rimland, B. (1982) "The altruism paradox," *Psychological Reports*, 51: 221–2.

Ross, W.D. (1930) *The Right and the Good*, Oxford: Clarendon Press.

Sartre, J-P. (1957) *Existentialism and Human Emotions*, New York: Wisdom Library.

Schulman, M., and Mekler, E. (1994) *Bringing Up a Moral Child*, New York: Doubleday.

Schwarz, S.D. (1990) *The Moral Question of Abortion*, Chicago: Loyola University Press.

Singer, M.G. (1963) "The golden rule," *Philosophy*, 38: 293–314.

Smart, J.C.C. (1967) "Utilitarianism," in the *Encyclopedia of Philosophy*.

Stevenson, C.L. (1963) *Facts and Values*, New Haven: Yale University Press.

Stowe, H.B. (1852) *Uncle Tom's Cabin*, New York: Harper & Row, 1965.

Sumner, W. (1911) *Folkways*, Boston: Ginn & Co.

Thomson, J.J. (1971) "A defense of abortion," *Philosophy and Public Affairs*, 1: 47–66.

Tooley, M. (1972) "Abortion and infanticide," *Philosophy and Public Affairs*, 2: 37–65.

Wattles, J. (1996) *The Golden Rule*, New York: Oxford University Press.

Werner, R. (1983) "Ethical realism," *Ethics*, 93: 653–79.

Index